Stories of Wil: Puberty Part 1

How Wil, who has Down syndrome,
entered his teenage years.

D1470512

Christie Taylor

To Elizabeth and Katherine,

sisters of gold

Foreword

Written by Lila Harvey, Wil's 13-year-old Friend

I have known Wil since Kindergarten. On the first day of
school we played an ice breaker game to get to know each
other. We went from person to person and said our names,
and favorite ice cream flavor. We got to choose who we
partnered up with. I chose Wil. He was shy and his
paraprofessional had to do most of the speaking for him but
that didn't bother me. I saw that he was different, but that
made me want to be friends with him. I never discriminated
against him. He was one of the reasons why I wanted to go to
school every day, just to see him. I sat with him almost every
day at lunch and tried to play with him at recess (sometimes he
didn't want to play). Then one day after school, I asked my
mom if I could have a playdate with Wil. My mom asked
"Who is Wil?" I told her he was a boy in my class who was
super nice. The next day, I introduced my mom to Wil. Then
my mom started to talk with Wil's mom and they hit it off. We
had the best playdate ever and we have had more playdates and
sleepovers than I can count.

Wil and I have become super close friends. It seems like every
time I am with Wil, we are always jamming out to either Luke
Bryan or Alan Jackson. Wil is always dancing and singing like
there is no tomorrow. He can be jamming away in class,
walking the track in gym, or having a dance party down in his
basement. He knows a lot more Luke Bryan songs than I do
and I always smile when I hear him singing. He could listen to
Luke Bryan till the end of the world if he can.

Wil IS different…

However, as different as he may be, I have always treated him like we were the same. When we were younger Wil and I went to a playground. We were going down one of the slides. I went down first and Wil was at the top. He wouldn't come down. I told him to get down the slide, but he was stubborn and wouldn't come down. Then I said, "Stop playing around Wil and get down here!" Wil realized that he couldn't fool me or get sympathy just because he was different so he came down. Just because he *is* different doesn't mean that I always treat him any differently than my other friends. Sometimes Wil does need a little extra help from his friends and when that happens we are always more than willing to support him as best we can.

Wil has bad days here and there. There have been some days when Wil just isn't in it. There have been a few times at lunch when he starts playing with his food or just sits in the hallway and doesn't want to do anything. Most of the time when this happens, Wil wants attention or he wants something. He is not the best at using his words, but he is getting better with it. His teachers and I are trying to get Wil to use his words at school. He is getting better each day with using his words, and I hope that one day, he won't be shy to say what he wants to say.

Now, every day I go to school to see Wil and get one of his awesome Wil Hugs. I never, ever have discriminated against Wil. He is one of my bestest friends in the entire world and I will never replace him. If I had the option, I would go back and do it all over again in a heartbeat.

Table of Contents

INTRODUCTION

Wil is a 13-year-old with Down syndrome. Wil's embarkment into teenage territory is the focus of this book. Wil is the younger brother, by 20 months, to twin sisters, Katherine and Elizabeth (yes, you did the math right—we have 3 teenagers in the house). Their dad, and my husband, is Matt. And I am their mother, Christie.

Now that Wil is a teenager, it's like we've crossed a proverbial bridge from the early days of navigating a brand new journey, into a new era full of hormones and more new behaviors. I've shared a few stories at the beginning of this book about our early days, as those stories laid the foundation of where we are on this journey now. However, the focus of this book is about crossing the proverbial bridge into teenage territory.

I suppose I should have known puberty would be challenging, but I was blindsided by the many behavioral changes that blossomed in Wil. Some of Wil's behaviors are attributed to having Down syndrome, while some are simply attributed to those good old hormones.

This is not a how-to book on coping with puberty in teenagers with Down syndrome. This is our story about puberty with Wil (we are still figuring out the how-to). My hope is, in sharing our story, that you will find yourself less blindsided than we did if you are about to embark into teenage territory. My hope is, if you are traversing similar territory, that we share a knowing smile as our stories cross paths. My hope is, if this journey is unfamiliar to you, that you gain a new level of understanding and appreciation for our amazing kids with Down syndrome along the way. I look forward to sharing more stories with you as we progress through this journey! Bon voyage!

OPENING STORY:
THIS IS HOW WE ROSE

I Am Not Grateful

I was not grateful when I learned Wil had Down syndrome.

I am not grateful my marriage was challenged by our differing timetables of acceptance.

I am not grateful my relationships with certain teachers have been strained by differing ideas of how to approach Wil's behaviors.

I am not grateful that I'm entering an era of hormones, girlfriends, and widening gaps within Wil's peer group.

I am not grateful for the stereotypes and ignorance my son will experience.

I do cry. I do get angry. I do get frustrated. I do things I regret. I am not grateful for these things.

I am grateful for a deeper level of acceptance I would not have known if Wil didn't have Down syndrome.

I am grateful my husband and I now share a deeper bond and respect for the challenges we worked through.

I am grateful that each day, month, and year I learn more about special education laws, advocacy, and the fact we are human and make mistakes.

I am grateful for second chances.

I am grateful that I have come to know a strong group of proactive parents I can laugh with and learn from. I am grateful to call these strong, compassionate people my friends.

I am grateful these experiences have compelled me to widen my perspective.

I am grateful for the advancement of acceptance so my son may have increased opportunities for a fulfilling life.

I am grateful I can contribute to the advancement of acceptance and increased opportunities.

I do smile. I do rejoice. I do feel joy. I do things I am proud of. I am grateful for these things.

I am grateful my gratitude creates a deeper well for the times I am not grateful.

NAVIGATING THE WATERS

Acing The Special Needs Test: Anyone Can Do It

"To raise someone with special needs takes someone special."

What does that mean exactly? Do I need a certain number of qualifications to be certified as special? Or was there some checklist I filled out? Who does the interviews anyway? I'm really confused as to how I qualified. I mean, I didn't ask for this. But I do have a son who has Down syndrome, and I love him. Does that make me qualified? We take creative routes sometimes. So does that qualify me as special? But don't you create the routes that you need to when you love somebody?

If only those of us who have passed some invisible test can raise a child with special needs, when will there be acceptance? I don't deny the challenges are there. I don't deny that we need to rise to an entirely new level of dedication. And I do revel in the inspiration I derive from other parents who do rise to such levels. But when it comes down to it, are any of us qualified as more special because we are doing what we need to for the love of our children? Isn't that what any parent would do? Would I do less for my child with special needs just because that journey looks different?

I was talking to a mother who has adopted multiple children with special needs. She is asked all the time how she does it. Her answer is: "We just do it. Anyone could do it."

There is a teenaged girl on our Challenger baseball team. She is in a wheelchair and has very little function in her arms and none in her legs. Her mother stands over her daughter's wheelchair at home plate, wraps her daughter's hands around the bat, and they both hit the ball as it's pitched to them. Her mother then grabs the back handles of her daughter's wheelchair and makes an all-out sprint to first base. Mother and daughter both laugh on their way there. When the next batter steps up, while the mother and daughter wait at first base, the mother makes conversation with her daughter. Her daughter, who is non-verbal, nods her head in response. They talk back and forth this way until the batter hits the ball. As this is Challenger baseball, and the kids all have varying levels of abilities, it may take some time before the ball is hit. Once the ball is hit, the mother once again makes a mad dash with her daughter, both laughing, to second base. This goes on until they make it to home plate. It's a joy to watch.

Do I find this situation inspiring? Absolutely. Do I think this mother is someone special? You betcha. But, here's the thing: this is their normal. This mother did not pass some kind of test or interview to be qualified as special. This mother is doing what she does because she loves her daughter. Her journey quite likely looks different than yours or mine. Her journey may be more challenging than yours or mine. But she loves her daughter just like you love your child and I love mine. This is the way they have fun and connect as mother and daughter, with all of the capabilities they have.

Our challenges and situations may look different, but when it comes down to it, we are all parents who love our kids. The love for our kids is special, and it lives inside of all of us—not just a select and qualified few. We are all doing the best we can, with the capabilities we have, in the villages we surround ourselves with.

We just do it. Anyone could do it.

All The Answers Of The World

The doctors suspected Wil had Down syndrome very shortly after his birth. The floor dropped out from under me. I grabbed tight to the sheets on my hospital bed, clinging to any sort of solid surface within reach. The questions swirled around me; I had so many. I fired them off to the doctor; I hoped I would stump him, that one of my questions would prove that Wil did not have Down syndrome. But the doctor had an answer for every single question I threw at him. Answers that pointed to Down syndrome. The only thing he couldn't confirm was the genetics test, which had a 72-hour turnaround time.

There were questions that the doctor couldn't answer, though. Questions that were not so black and white. Questions like: What does this diagnosis mean for my son's quality of life? How will this diagnosis affect my marriage? How will this diagnosis affect my daughters? How will this diagnosis affect my son's friendships? Will my son be able to drive, go to college, go to work, live independently, get married, have children? What happens when I'm gone? Who will take care of him? I desperately craved the answers to these questions.

As I navigated the various therapy and doctor appointments in Wil's first months of life, the questions grew. Just as the questions grew, however, so did my relationships with the therapists and doctors. I met many families who were also raising children with Down syndrome and we became friends. The questions no longer stood out in front of me, but walked beside me.

Certain answers unfolded in front of me, in time, as I navigated my way. While other questions remained unanswered, walking with me side-by-side, I no longer felt the dizzying abyss below. I had found my footing, even without all of the answers. I realized that on this new path, I would always have new questions, but I could fully enjoy the walk anyway. I found myself paying more attention to my surroundings than I ever had before. And those who walked this path with me did the same. It was a beautiful experience to share.

Now that I've been walking this path for 13 years with Wil, I've watched the gap widen between his abilities and those of his peers. I see it in the classroom... I see it on the playground... I see it on the soccer field... I see it in the swimming pool. It's everywhere he is with those typically-developing peers. They move faster, they talk faster, and they are becoming interested in teenage topics. They are doing what teenagers do. The questions are there: how can I explain these changes to Wil in a way he will understand? How can I make these relationships mutually beneficial?

An unexpected diagnosis may leave us grasping for answers. But I have learned one thing: the questions never go away. They change with time. I have learned to walk with these ever-changing questions along the way. Time will reveal the answers to some of them. Asking more questions, reaching out to friends, hearing friends share their experiences, and trial and error will bring more answers. And some questions I will need to learn to walk with for the time being. Questions are part of the journey. But they are not the whole of it.

The whole of this journey is all that I've discovered on this new path and all that is to come. The whole of this journey is made in our relationships and our daily growth—be it in baby steps, or leaps and bounds, or somewhere in between. The whole of this journey is ever-changing, challenging, joyful, and giving. The whole of this journey is one I'd never trade for all the answers of the world.

Overwhelmed

We walked down the hallway of the church, where the meeting was being held. Matt held the baby carrier, which was swaying slightly with the gait of his walk. It was somewhat dim in the hallway, and Matt's and my footfalls were echoing off the walls. It was evening, and the congregation had long since returned home from the morning's service.

Though this was the first time we had set foot inside this church, I imagined the vibration of the organ's music under my feet, the choir in white robes—a bright satin sash of solid color draped diagonally across their chests. White candles being lit, the rise of the preacher behind the pulpit, singing along heartily with his choir—his flock forgiving his tone deafness for his heart for his Lord.

The sound of voices ahead broke the reverie of the imaginary church service in my mind. The mind is a master of distraction. For that brief moment of choir-filled distraction, I was thankful. My mind had been a swirl of unanswered questions since our son was born just over a month ago. I felt I was living in some kind of surreal dream, thoughts swirling like Picasso clouds above my head. A cloud is a cloud, and yet... different.

Matt and I followed the sound of voices and found ourselves in a very typical church classroom. Spacious, rectangular, utilitarian. An oblong table had been constructed with two or three long tables pushed next to each other on each side of the room, with one long table connecting the ends of both sides. The tables were lined with chairs. No one was sitting. Women stood around the outskirts of the table, along with a few men (I was relieved to see for Matt). People were clustered in small groups of four or five. But they didn't stay in their groups. They would mingle and move around from group to group. There was a sense of ease about them—they all knew one another. To the far right of the room was an open area. About ten children ran around laughing and playing. Tears started streaming down my face. I couldn't even place emotions for what I was feeling—it was all jumbled up inside of me. If I had to scoop it all up in my arms and label it, I'd call it "overwhelm." I was "overwhelmed."

There were a few adults in this area too, chatting with one another, playing with the kids—or redirecting a child from taking off toward a door. It all seemed so normal, but it wasn't.

"Hi, have we met before?" A woman was standing in front of me.

"Oh! Um, I'm sorry, I just… um, we are the Taylors. I'm Christie. This is my husband, Matt, and um, this is our little guy, Wil. He's just over a month old now. We have twin girls too. They're home with my mother-in-law right now."

"Very nice to meet you, I'm so glad you came," she said, and put her arm around my shoulder. "Let me introduce you to some parents."

When things don't *feel* normal inside, the simplest normal responses are breathed in deep like the fresh air they are. I don't remember all of the people Matt and I met, but we met almost everyone in that room. The common theme, over and over, was "yes, this is a challenging journey, but a very joyful and gratifying one. Though you may not see it now, you will. I promise, I promise." I didn't see as far into the journey as they did, but their promises were my beacon. Though I didn't grasp the full meaning of their statements, I could now see beyond the blur of surreal clouds I was living in, heavy with question marks.

Soon, the meeting began and we all sat down in the chairs that lined the oblong table. The majority of the meeting was about learning styles for our kids. Before Wil had even reached 2 months old, I discovered that day that our kids with Down syndrome are mainly visual learners and math tended to be the most challenging subject. I don't remember many other details about the sit-down portion of that meeting. However, I did take home one key element: questions are good, but you can also get too far ahead of yourself. I wanted to know everything, right now. I wanted those funky, surreal clouds to disappear and the answers to make themselves known. And they would, in time. In time I would learn about Wil's math skills. In time I would learn about Wil's visual learning. But right then, I realized that what I most needed was having my feelings validated. For someone to say, you know what, I was there too. For someone to say, yes, you have a beautiful baby, but it's also okay to feel sad, to feel scared, to feel like you don't know what is happening. For someone to say, we have tried to decipher the same Picasso clouds too, and we have walked through them, and we promise—and promise again—the sun is shining on the other side. It may be a Picasso sun, but you will appreciate this type of sun more for having known the Picasso clouds.

Time is hugely discomfiting as you wait for answers. And that is exactly why time is also a healer. Some things must happen with time. With experience. With day-to-day learning. Living in the unknown is an unsettling place to be. I thought knowing the answers would heal my pain. But it was the time with my son, and experiences with him, that opened my eyes to the beauty of our new landscape.

On the last Sunday of September each year, I walk into a big park for our Down Syndrome Support Team's annual Buddy Walk (an event to raise funds and awareness for individuals with Down syndrome). Some years there is sunshine. Some years there are clouds. And some years there is rain. But every year, you will find multiple volunteers assembling long rows of tables lined with chairs. A big truck will pull up and unpack banners, balloons, t-shirts, food trays, and such. Another big truck will arrive with a stage and band equipment. Once the stage, instruments, and speakers are set up, the music begins to play. There are many spare instruments laid out for anyone

15

who would like to play with the band. It doesn't take long before a huge group of kids and adults, with and without Down syndrome, are dancing and playing with the band. There are multiple families and friends clustered around the stage. They mingle and move around and talk with one another. There is a sense of ease about them—even if they don't know one another, they all have a common bond that brings them together.

This is a surreal dream. One that I now can't imagine not living in. Those funky Picasso clouds and sun I once wondered about are our normal. The promises I held so tightly to those years ago *did* come true. Time, experience, and support truly are healers. If I had to scoop it all up in my arms and label it, I'd still call it "overwhelm." I am overwhelmed with joy, gratitude, fortitude, and community.

Step One Is One Step

After coaching an early morning fitness class, I was talking to one of the members. I asked her what her occupation was. She told me she was a social worker. I never knew much about social workers until Wil was born.

"You do good work," I said, "but my guess is a lot of people don't see it that way. They probably don't want to see you at all." A social worker came into my hospital room the afternoon after Wil was born and she was the last person I wanted to see.

"Yes, I can walk into some very challenging situations." She went on to tell me about some of her cases, keeping confidentiality.

When I was struggling with Wil's diagnosis shortly after his birth, I was wary of that social worker who walked through the door of my hospital room. My first thought was that she would try to fix me. That she would try to tell me that everything was going to be ok and that I could do this. I had learned of my son's diagnosis only hours ago, and I was emotionally spent at that time. I couldn't think past the next minute—let alone open myself to the suggestions of someone who didn't know me.

That's why I'm not particularly fond of the posts on social media proclaiming, "You are awesome!" "I believe in you!" "You can do it!" While these are kind and positive messages, they have no specificity. These messages do not connect to a situation with substantial meaning. If the social worker walked into my hospital room and said, "You can do it!" I would have asked, "Do what, exactly? How about you tell me how I can get through the next minute?" Conversely if she said, "Today, I'm going to ask that you take a shower. Take as long of a shower as you need to," I would have jumped out of bed and hugged her. Taking a shower was a specific action—one that would have helped cut through my fog of thoughts at the time.

When living in a fog of overwhelm, one specific direction is enough to get the ball rolling in the direction of "You can do it!" The social worker who walked into my room, though, did not make any vague statements or give me any specific actions to take. She didn't placate me, try to fix me, or tell me everything was going to be alright. She was much smarter than that. She didn't say anything at all. Rather, she stood at the end of my hospital bed and held up a folder for me to see. The edges of the folder were a deep, bright royal blue. The focus of the folder was an enlarged, close-up picture of a blond girl with Down syndrome holding a flower. Her eyes were even brighter and deeper than the blue of the folder. "Isn't she beautiful?" The social worker asked me. Then she waited for my response.

This experience happened over 13 years ago, and every time I remember it, my eyes well with tears. When I recounted this story to the social worker at the gym, it was no different. Impactful moments do not lose their emotional power easily.

Not a single person told us our baby was beautiful the morning of his birth. His birth was, instead, a flurry of activity. Within seconds of hearing, "It's a boy," a nurse declared my baby was "floppy." Elation made way to confusion in seconds. I asked what floppy meant. The nurse told me it meant low muscle tone. And low muscle tone usually meant Down syndrome. Soon a doctor came in and confirmed that Wil had short stubby fingers, separation in his toes, and small nasal passages. More signs of Down syndrome.

By the afternoon of Wil's birth, when I laid alone in the hospital bed while he was being examined, the words I most needed to hear came from the person I least wanted to see— the social worker who walked, uninvited by me, into my room. My preconceived notions of her purpose there were shattered. The social worker helped me see past the moment I was in. She was a beacon in the fog. She gifted me not only a forward step, but a giant leap into "You can do it!" with three powerful words.

In Wil's first months, I began to seek out support groups. I went to a number of meetings with various different groups, all of which *did* validate the pain of the initial shock. They all knew the fog I was finding my way through. However, some stayed in that cloudy place. They told their sad stories, and everyone listened. But what was missing was how to get out of the clouds. I didn't want empty promises of positivity. But I also didn't want to stay where I was. I craved the beacon the social worker gave me. I walked out the door of those groups, thanked them for their time, and never went back.

A few years ago, Matt and I went to marriage counseling. On our first visit, when the counselor was navigating our situation, she asked me if I felt I was to blame for birthing a child with Down syndrome. I was flabbergasted. That never once crossed my mind. Down syndrome is random, and in any case, what good does blame do? I had learned over the years that I was the center of my story. That no matter what anyone did to me, I was still the center. That I had the choice—to decide to make my life better, or to wallow in pain. She ended up being a very helpful counselor, but her question always stayed with me. It was a reminder to never get stuck in useless blame. The marriage counselor gifted me another forward step.

The reason Matt and I went to marriage counseling is because we each came to accept Wil's Down syndrome at a different rate. No one person comes to acceptance in the same way and at the same time. Acceptance is a journey of experiences. In this journey, it's helpful to walk side-by-side with others, but you also must do your own work. Matt and I had our own separate work to do so that we could come together in acceptance. We are different people with different backstories. We work well together, but we often see and approach experiences in different ways. Matt and I needed help in bringing our levels of acceptance together for the sake of our marriage, for the sake of Wil, and for the sake of Katherine and Elizabeth. We are their role models in how to value acceptance of differences.

It's not something that can be answered with vague, positive messages. This process cannot be helped along with a blanket, "You can do it!" It's about validating each other's specific needs and concerns. Some days it's a high-five and other days it's a kick in the pants. It's a one-step-at-a-time kind of process.

In the early days after Wil's birth, many helpful family members and friends gave me phone numbers of acquaintences who had a child with Down syndrome. "Here, call them!" they said. The thought behind these passed on phone numbers was one of kindness. And the meaning behind them was one of wanting to help. And yet here you are, feeling overly emotional, and there is so much information being thrown at you at once you don't even know where to start. Calling a complete stranger can feel absolutely monumental in the moment.

I now get asked if I'd be willing to talk to a mother who just birthed a child with Down syndrome. I love nothing more than to be approached to talk to their friend or family member. I too want to help and be supportive. But I remember those early days well. I always agree to my contact information being passed on. But I also add, "let them know they can email me or text if that's easier. It's never too early or too late to reach out to me. Sometimes one phone call can feel absolutely overwhelming. I'm here when *they* are ready." One step at a time.

Sometimes making one single phone call to a stranger is all you have in you. One step. Sometimes taking a shower that day is downright heroic. One step. Sometimes working up the courage to approach your spouse about the accruing months of differing rates of acceptance is the most monumental thing you can do. One step.

When you can't see further than today, committing to one, specific step is the bravest thing you can do. One step-one step-one step. Is that royal blue I see on the edges of the fog? One step-one step-one step. I see blue eyes. One step-one step-one step. The full picture is coming into view. It is a different picture than I expected. One step-one step-one step. Oh, would you look at that. Now that I've stepped up, and I can see clearly now, the beauty is spectacular.

Time

I sat at the kitchen table, my chair turned slightly outward—toward the kitchen sink, where Matt stood, washing dishes. Miraculously, Katherine, Elizabeth, and Wil were all in one of the bedrooms playing together. This is the time, I thought.

"Matt, what is it that you need?" I asked him. He stopped, holding a plate, the water running over it. He looked at me, then looked back to the plate, the water continuing to run down its surface. I said to myself, "shut up shut up, shut up. Let him think. Don't interrupt his train of thought with words." The exaggerated pause went on, and I willed myself to stay quiet. I knew the wheels were turning in his head.

We had been married long enough for me to know how his mind worked. When I was growing up, if you paused what you were saying, the person you were talking to assumed you were done with that thought, and filled the space with *their* words. If you weren't done with your thought, you'd circle back around to it, if you felt it important enough to do so.

With Matt, there are a lot of pauses. He thinks through his words carefully—a phrase, a thought, and another phrase. When Matt and I were first married, I didn't understand his pauses. I assumed he was done with his thought and it was my turn to respond, and so I did. I soon learned that when I did that, Matt would *not* circle back, so I never fully heard his full view on a subject. So now, with this understanding I'd gained over the years, I reminded myself to remain quiet. I really, really wanted to hear his thoughts on what I was asking. Though at the moment, as much as I wanted to hear him talk, I wasn't exactly appreciating waiting. I was tired of waiting. I had moved on and I wanted him to move on too. But he was on one side and I was on another. The pause went on, the water still running. I couldn't take it anymore.

"Matt?" I asked.

"Time," he said.

Katherine and Elizabeth were born in June 2005 and Wil followed about 20 months later, in February 2007. In the 20-month span before Wil was born, I carefully laid out Katherine and Elizabeth's first words in their baby books. I delicately inserted their first locks of cut hair with details on their experience. I wrote out their sleeping habits, what their favorite toys were, how I enjoyed the fact that their astrological sign was also that of twins (Gemini), and what was happening in the world at large—who the president was (George double-ya), the current weather, the fashion and popular songs of the time. Hardly a detail was missed—I filled in every pause.

Now, Katherine and Elizabeth circle back to read the memories of their early lives. Though their first 20 months spanned an eventful time, the 72 hours after Wil's birth threatened to hang above my head like a stagnant cloud. I was told it would take 72 hours for a genetics test to confirm the suspicions that Wil had Down syndrome. How could I wait an eternity to confirm a diagnosis? This 3-day pause in time was more than I could bear. I pleaded for an answer. I desperately needed to move on and know what our situation was. The 72-hour cloud hung heavy above me—the answer was on one side of it and I was on the other.

Finally, after much pleading on my part, one doctor confirmed that Wil had all the signs of having Down syndrome. I was given folders about Down syndrome the very afternoon after Wil's birth. A social worker also came to visit me that same afternoon. Family members came in and cried. Though the cloud had shifted forward, it still hung heavy in front of me, blocking my view of the future. In fact, I could hardly see past today. But at least I had a definition to look at. By the time the 72 hours came and we received official confirmation, it was simply a formality. However, I did learn that Wil had Trisomy 21—the most common form of Down syndrome. In a strange way, even though I was struggling with the diagnosis, learning of the commonality of Wil's type of Down syndrome that day was a stroke of relief in a sea of bewilderment. Though I felt as if I was standing on an unknown island at the time, I discovered this island was well-populated. I may have been lost, but I no longer felt alone.

I tried to nurse Wil, but with his low muscle tone, he needed lots of time and attention to get the nutrition he needed. With Katherine and Elizabeth not even 2 years old yet, I didn't have the luxury of time to sit still, let alone to take the hours needed to help Wil nurse properly. Wil's weight was dropping, as he wasn't getting the nutrition he needed. He would only accept bottles with the disposable nipples from the hospital. Would not nursing Wil set him back? He was already born with cognitive and physical delays. His immune system was already compromised. I asked his pediatrician how much I would be setting him back if I changed to bottles and formula (when I explained my situation with Wil only accepting the hospital bottles, a kind nurse gave me a large garbage bag full of individually packaged disposable nipples). Of course, the pediatrician said that nursing was best, but so was getting Wil the nutrition he needed. He asked me to hang on for 6 weeks if I could. That's what I did, then went to bottles with the disposable nipples and formula—so I knew exactly the nutrition Wil was getting, and didn't have to spend hours trying to nurse him and keep Katherine and Elizabeth occupied at the same time.

Wil was gaining weight and growing. The 6 weeks I nursed Wil was both an eternity of patience and a blur of activity. When it was over, and I changed him to 100% bottles and formula, I didn't realize how stressed I had been over that decision. I let out a deep breath and reveled in the pause in time, then moved on fully from one side to the other.

I began to grow a village around me. The first was Early On— an early intervention program for children birth to age 3. I met the therapists—speech, occupational, and physical—who came to our home and worked with Wil. They showed me exercises to do with Wil, and also included Katherine and Elizabeth, who were very intrigued with Wil's therapies and liked to help out. The therapists in those early days gave me hope, even if they couldn't give me concrete answers.

I asked the physical therapist if Wil would walk. She answered that he would, but could not say when. Maybe he would be 2 years old, maybe he would be 5. I sat there again, the stagnant cloud heavy above me. I was on one side of that question, the answer on the other. Though this time, there was no test that would give me a black and white answer. Time would tell. I was desperate to fill the pause. I willed myself to be patient. Finally, I could take no more. I asked the physical therapist again, in different ways.

The physical therapist could give me no concrete answer, but in response, she asked me a question: "See how Wil walks on a balance beam?"

Wil walked on the balance beam, with the therapist holding his right hand on one side of the beam, and me holding his left hand on the other.

"See how he can put one foot in front of the other, even though he's not able to walk on his own yet?" She asked.

"Yes," I responded.

"Well, he's not supposed to be able to do that. But he is. Sometimes kids are expected to be able to do A and B before they can do C. But Wil, well, he does A then C. Eventually he will circle back to B. That's just how he does things."

In this way, I learned to be patient in the pauses—to not fill in the spaces, but to wait for Wil to do that in his own time. I was then able to delight in celebrating when he achieved the "C" activity, even if we would have to circle back for him to complete the "B" activity. Progress is progress, no matter how many times we had to circle back to move forward.

Wil now runs, jumps, and swims. He can jump rope like a champ. He also just celebrated the first birthday of his teenage years. Wil still puts "C" before "B." Some days make sense and some days don't. Deciphering a certain behavior Wil is exhibiting can feel like an eternity, while other times the triggers of his behaviors are clear.

It's easy to step into a situation, point fingers and say, "she should have done this," or "he could have done that." But what is deemed as "right" is not always what is right for *our* situation. That is exactly why I love my special island of Trisomy 21 families. We know what works today has a really good chance of not working tomorrow. This journey is about willing ourselves to shut up so the door may open for someone else to be heard. This journey is about the constant asking of questions—knowing there may not be a direct answer, but that it's worth asking questions anyway, because we know the answers will come in their own way. This journey requires holding strong in every pause with all the proactive and patient energy we have. This journey is about leap-frogging two steps ahead and circling back to pick up the one you hopped over. This journey is about letting go of guilt, because what is deemed right is not always right for the situation. This journey is about celebrating every single step, as jagged and zig-zaggy as the road may be. I can't promise that this journey will always make sense. But I can promise that this journey will be worth every moment of your time.

GROWING WITH WIL

Open

When I opened the car door, I felt the wind hit my face. I instinctively braced myself in defense. I then looked over to see Wil step out of the passenger side of the car. When he felt the wind, he tilted his face to the sky, opened his arms wide, and spun around in circles, allowing the wind to propel him. I watched him in awe, then followed his lead, opening myself to the wind.

Look At Me, Mom

"Look at me, Mom." He took my hands and placed them on either side of his face. What he took my attention from screamed for it back. I did not have time to look at him. But as I did, he smiled. I melted, and his face made everything else fade to the background. His almond-shaped blue eyes, his soft, yet direct, stare that asks for all that I am. He wanted the whole of his mom's attention. A portion of that would not do.

Most of us desire the whole attention of whoever we are with, but many of us are not bold enough to ask. We rarely even ask that of ourselves—living lives with our attention divided amongst multiple simultaneous directions. And still, he never forgets to ask. Thank goodness. Whenever he asks, I am brought back to life. The whole of my life. Back to a place I didn't know I lost because I was so busy being elsewhere. My hands on his face made life zoom into a clear and singular focus. The feeling is incredibly freeing. I am filled with the peace, love, and focus I was born with, but that had clouded over in the increasing busyness of each year that passed.

This same feeling of peace returns to us when we hold our newborn babies. We can stare at their sweet, innocent faces, with their gurgles and giggles and their sleep for hours. Everything else fades to the background. They are our everything. Then they start crawling, and soon are toddling and pulling themselves up to a stand. They take their first uncertain steps. Though they are still our everything, distractions start finding their way into the periphery. Our children soon inherit the habit of distraction just as we did. The habit is formed from observing our parents… from our environment… from responsibility that comes with age. This habit is formed very gradually and we don't even notice it happening. Our life feels full—full because it is full of busyness.

Then one day, an awakening happens. This awakening typically arrives in a simple way because that is how the true joys of life are. Simple.

When Wil placed my hands on his face, I was washing dishes. I stood at the sink, my mind a million miles away, focused on the million other things that I had to do and what I already had done. His voice cut through the galaxy of my thoughts. "Look at me, Mom." When he took my hands and placed them on his face, they were like paddles shocking me back to life. My life was kicked back into rhythm with what matters. This moment was not another distraction covering up the other distractions, such as a drink, or a drug, or food. This moment was when my mind shut up and listened to the whole of what my son had to say.

The Good Fight

I believe in the ultimate value of acceptance. I believe in the good fight for acceptance. I also believe in a time for good peace. A time of rejuvenation. It's summertime, after all.

Wil will transition to a new school in the fall, but in the same school district. While there will be many changes, staying in the same district should make the transition smoother. He will enjoy being with many of his friends, but he will have a new resource room, a new resource room teacher, some new and some familiar teachers for his general education classes, and a new paraprofessional. The school will be much larger. With his budding independence, he may enjoy a larger school—or he may find it overwhelming.

When Wil entered kindergarten, I was in the good fight mode. He had come from a very nurturing preschool environment, and I enjoyed constant communication with his teachers. I was nervous about the multitude of changes that his being in a new school for a full day would bring. How would his teachers know all of his capabilities? Many of the tests he had taken that measured his skills didn't accurately show what he could do. His new therapists and teachers wouldn't have an adequate picture of where to start with him, and I wouldn't be able to communicate with them until a full day of school had been completed.

I learned during this transition that being in the same school district had its benefits. That though many aspects of his day had changed, the preschool teachers communicated with the kindergarten teachers. The holes the tests didn't fill in were communicated from preschool to kindergarten via person-to-person dialogue. I now know the same will happen as Wil transitions to his new school in the fall.

I recently talked to a mother who has a young child with Down syndrome. She is in the good fight mode—full of vigor for her fight for inclusion with her child's school. I listened to her with admiration, and remembered our early days. There were many unknowns. There still are many unknowns where I currently stand, but they are different.

Wil has been in this district from preschool through 6th grade. I know we will have hurdles to cross next year. We always do. We will handle those hurdles on a day-to-day basis as they come. Then, when the next transition to young adulthood comes, we will tackle new hurdles. I don't yet know what those hurdles will be, but we will again get in good fight mode and make our way through. But right now, it's summertime. My grass is green and free of hurdles—I want to dig my toes in and enjoy it while it lasts. Inclusion is not a given, and the good fight always lies ahead. But it is also just as important to know when a time of good peace is upon you. To breathe it in and enjoy the fresh, wide-open moment you're in.

Every Thursday in the summertime, Wil attends Special Olympics golf. Every Thursday is also a reminder to be thankful for the opportunities Wil has in life. I'm eternally grateful for those who stepped up to the good fight and created Special Olympics when nothing of its kind existed. I'm eternally thankful to the volunteers and participants who continue to grow this powerful program. When Wil and I walk down the road to meet our friends at Special Olympics every Thursday, we walk a road that was paved by those fighting the good fight. They paved the way so we may enjoy a time of good peace.

Progress comes with our good fight, and our hearts regain their well of strength during times of good peace. Families raising children with special needs live with the knowledge of the good fight nearly every day—it becomes ingrained. Meeting the young mother who is currently in the midst of a good fight reminded me of that. All of life is a balance. We gain strength from both the good fight and the good peace. This summer, I am breathing this time of good peace in deep. I do not know what the fall will bring when school begins, but I will be refreshed and recharged to build or cross that bridge when the time comes.

I Remember When

When? That was my favorite question in the beginning. Even if it was not always specifically answerable, the question of "when" held a note of hope. "When" promises it *will* happen—it's only the timeline that is unclear. On one occasion, I asked the question, "will he?" I was answered with a long pause. Like "when," the question of "will he" is also not specifically answerable. However, "will he?" holds no promises. In the beginning, there are already too many unanswered questions. Even the slightest indication of hope is a source of strength.

There may be no such thing as a bad question, but there is such a thing as a better question. I was already living with too many question marks; I didn't want to ask for more. I quickly learned to ask questions that had an answer with a hint of hope. I didn't have to have all the answers, I only needed to know there was an opportunity to aim for. That was enough.

I didn't know if Wil would talk. Nobody knew. At first I asked "will he?" No one could answer that question. I rephrased that as, "when will he?" Though I received no definitive answer, I did receive a more proactive one. As in, "if we try this, then..." "When?" looks ahead. "Will he?" stands there and wonders.

Wil's first words were a thrill. Like any baby, he babbled. Like any mother, I heard decipherable words in his babble. The question was, when would two words come? Two words were much greater than one. Two words meant comprehension. Two words meant that three words would come. Three words meant that sentences would come. Three words meant that he could communicate with others. Three words meant four- and five-word sentences would come. Complete sentences meant he could have a conversation. The ability to have a conversation meant he could talk together with friends. Talking with friends meant the ability to create a fuller social life. Having a fuller social life meant the ability to having an enriching life. Having an enriching life meant the ability to contribute to society and be fulfilled in his adulthood. My mind jumped ahead to the possibilities.

Wil started in one-word sentences. He'd ask for a Goldfish cracker by saying, "Goldfish." When that sentence expanded to, "Goldfish, Mom," I felt as if streamers and balloons would fall from the sky in celebration. Months upon months of speech therapy were behind those two words coming together in beautiful harmony. Each and every new word was a victory. Not a single word ever missed or taken for granted. The question of "when?" was answered. It was answered on its own timeline, but it was answered nonetheless.

Wil has been talking in complete sentences for years now, and I continue to thrill at the formation of any new additional word. I don't miss a single one. Each word breaks way to a new hope. Each word holds the strength of forward progress. My first questions were the building blocks of our new hopes and dreams.

Recently, Wil looked up at the sunset and pointed. "Mom, look," he said. "The sunset is beautiful." "Yes it is, Wil," I responded, as my heart filled to capacity with the fullness of his sentences. "Not nearly as beautiful as your words used to show it to me," I thought to myself. "Because I remember when."

Discovering New Stars

When Wil was a baby, I declared he would have full inclusion in the classroom throughout his school years, earn a high school diploma, and go on to college.

Wil is now a teenager. I continue to hold high hopes for him, though my declarations now look different. Wil will not earn a high school diploma—he will earn a Certificate of Completion. I do have every expectation that Wil will take adapted college courses. Wil is in the 7th grade and is reading at a 2nd grade level. When he was a baby, that may have been hard for me to accept; I may have believed someone wasn't doing their job. Now I know all the hard work that went behind Wil reading at his current level. When I see Wil sit on the couch and read a book or pick up a menu, read it, and order for himself, I couldn't be prouder.

There is no way I could have known those 13 years ago what the steps to get Wil where he is today would look like. I had to take those steps with him, one day after another. My early high hopes for Wil were very important. They were stars to reach for. As we made our way down the path toward those very stars, I realized some realigning of our constellations would need to be done. Wil works hard—when he wants to—but no matter how hard he works, the reality is that he processes words slower than his typical peers. Having low muscle tone means he moves slower than they do. As Wil grew older, it became clear he did his best learning with math and reading in his resource room, rather than the general education classroom. In the resource room, Wil has one-on-one attention and works at a pace that best suits his individual learning style. He is also learning life skills there, such as cooking and counting money.

Wil has full inclusion in gym, science, and social studies. Now that he's going through puberty, every morning is a true test. He needs lots and lots of encouragement to get out of bed—if there's any forcing him, his whole day could be set back. It's hard emotionally, for me. Every morning I need to steel myself for the long haul. For no missteps.

I know we will get through this. But right now, it's hard. I'm entering a new chapter with Wil. I relate it to when he was born. I'm navigating a new place I have not been before. When Wil was born, I wanted to know what Down syndrome was all about. I could read about Down syndrome, but I didn't have a full understanding until I l took those first steps down this new path. Now I'm navigating "What is Down syndrome with Puberty?" I'm traveling alongside other parents on this very path. As we are entering new territory, I find it extremely valuable to walk with others who understand not just what this experience looks like, but what it *feels* like.

Puberty is a challenging experience for anyone. Add communication and comprehension barriers to that mix, and it's a whole new learning experience. Right now I can best equate it to a tall-hedged maze. I can't see where we're going, or what direction to turn in, but I know we will eventually make our way through. We walk down one aisle to find a dead end. We walk backwards, retrace our steps to where we were, and try a new direction. We hit another dead end. We walk backwards again, start over, move forward and find ourselves further ahead this time than before. We will build on that progress, advance a little further, and find another dead end— but this time we'll know we are closer to making our way through. We'll try again. And again.

Never dismiss the power of a 13-year-old boy reading at a 2nd grade level. This achievement is not behind, but right on time, for the emotional strength and steps taken to arrive in this very place. We continue to walk our path reaching for the stars, but in a different way than we started out. In the beginning, I believed that high stars were declared, then set in place. But somewhere along the way, I realized that the constellations need rearranging, again and again. Even so, they continue to brightly light our path. And the light doesn't just come from the sky. True stars walk beside me—the ones I have emotional connections with, that walk with me along the same mazy path.

Shared Smiles

There is something about people with Down syndrome that makes strangers smile. And not just one type of smile. I've recognized varying degrees of smiles.

There is the "warm, friendly smile." This type comes from those who have an acquaintance with Down syndrome or a positive image of people with Down syndrome.

There is the "he's-so-darn-adorable smile." Because Wil is so darn adorable and adorable kids make it easy to smile.

There is the "sympathy smile." This smile comes with a look of concern. First, Wil is looked at with concern, then the "sympathy smiler" looks up at me with sadness in their eyes.

There is the "knowing smile"—my absolute favorite. The "knowing smiler" looks at Wil longer than the typical smiler, with a far off daze appearing in their eyes. It's as though looking at Wil has transported the "knowing smiler" somewhere else, and I can feel an immediate connection. When they look up at me, their smile says "I know you even though we haven't met before." Sometimes they will share a story with me about their loved one with Down syndrome. Sometimes they won't. Either way, I know by their smile. They love somebody with Down syndrome deep down in their heart. It's a beautiful connection, if only through a smile.

Happy Is As Happy Does

I hadn't been feeling very well. Wil had just got over the flu, and I may have contracted a lesser degree of his illness. I had decided to sleep in that morning, and Matt had left for work long before I woke up. I could smell the coffee in the kitchen when I awoke—the fact that it smelled good was a sign I was on the mend. I love coffee, but had felt nauseous drinking it the day before. Katherine, Elizabeth, and Wil were still sleeping. On my way into the kitchen, I walked by our dog Woody, who was curled up in his bed on the living room floor. He didn't lift his head, but his tail, extending past the outskirts of his round bed, gently and rhythmically tapped the hardwood floor with a gentle thump, thump, thump. I bent down to give him a pet.

I then poured myself a cup of coffee and turned the desk light on just above the Lazy Boy chair and nestled in with a book. My New Year's resolution was to stay off of any type of media first thing in the morning and to read an uplifting book.

Soon I heard Wil rustling in his bed. He must have gotten up and seen the light on in the living room. He peeked through the doorway in his room. As soon as he saw me, he quickly stood back upright and shut his door. Privacy had been a big deal lately.

A few minutes later, he emerged fully dressed in a button-up collared shirt and pants.

"Going somewhere special today, Wil?" I asked.

"Hi, Mom."

"Hi, Wil."

He walked over and cuddled up in the Lazy Boy with me.

"You are squishing me, Mom."

"Hey, I was here first, you stinker. I think it's you that is squishing me."

"Oh, Mom. You are being silly."

I imagine that my hearing Wil speak in full sentences is how an elementary music teacher must feel when her young, budding choir finally comes together in harmony. There are hours of practice behind putting the melody together. Wil used to say, "You be silly Mom." Now, it is a beautiful, "You are being silly." "Ugh, squished" has expanded to, "You are squishing me, Mom." Those elongated sentences are a symphony to this mother's ears.

"Breakfast now, Mom."

"Ok, let's have your pill first." Wil has had hypothyroidism since he was six months old. This is very common in individuals with Down syndrome.

"Do you want to get out the peanut butter this morning, or me?" I asked him. (Wil prefers to take his pill in a spoonful of peanut butter).

"I get the peanut butter."

After I scooped peanut butter on his spoon and sunk the pill into it, I held it up to his mouth. His independence may be growing, but with his pill, he still loves the game of "open the tunnel." He took the spoon, I said "open the tunnel," and he swallowed down his pill.

"Mom, guess what. I'm a choo-choo train!" He started taking straight-legged, tiny steps around the kitchen island. His arms were bent at 90 degrees, making short, choppy swings.

"Mom, you do it with me!" I fell in with my own straight-legged, tiny steps behind Wil and we choo-chooed around the island.

Once we had made it full circle, he laughed and said, "Ok, done now."

Wil helped me make his two breakfast sandwiches of ham, cheese, spinach, and honey mustard sauce on whole wheat buns. Then he grabbed his plate and walked downstairs to watch *Sofia the First* on Netflix. I don't know why, but he only watches that show while he eats. When he's done eating, he's done watching and moves on to something else to play with. I returned to reading on the Lazy Boy.

When Wil came upstairs after eating his breakfast, the sun was rising and warm on the window in the living room. He leaned his back up against the glass and said, "Ahhhh warm. It's a beautiful day, Mom."

"Yes, it is. Elizabeth has basketball practice this morning, but when she gets back, let's go outside."

"Ok, Mom."

Wil walked off to his room and put his favorite Luke Bryan CD in his CD player. He started singing at the top of his lungs. I walked into his room and started singing with him.

"No, Mom. Just me this time." (I again heard the symphony with the addition of "this time," as he used to say "just me.")

"Oh, fine," I said and rolled my eyes. "You never let me have any fun."

"Oh, Mom, you are being silly."

I gave him a hug and went back to my book. He restarted the song, because clearly I had messed up his groove. But I still belted out the song's chorus with him from the Lazy Boy because I just couldn't help myself.

When you haven't been feeling well, you never appreciate the feeling of being healthy again more than when you weren't. Coffee smelled and tasted good again, my dog greeted me with the thump of his tail, and I was living up to my resolution of reading and staying off of media in the morning. Wil and I had choo-chooed around the kitchen, and now music was happening. When Katherine and Elizabeth woke up, I would surely annoy them with my great enthusiasm for the day.

Happiness isn't always this remote object that hangs in the ethers that chooses when to befall us. Happiness also isn't merely positive thinking— it's also positive *doing*. Happiness is feeling good because you feel good. Happiness is creating a game out of the task of a daily pill. Happiness is leaning into the warmth of the morning sun on your window. Happiness is hearing a symphony in a string of words. Happiness is singing at the top of your lungs simply because you can. Happiness is always there in what we do, feel, hear, say, and sing.

Hash Brown Robbery

I'm sharing this experience for those of you who believe children with Down syndrome have not a single mean bone in their body. You may want to rethink that after reading the following story.

I woke Wil up early for a routine doctor's appointment. I promised him a McDonald's breakfast afterwards as added motivation to get up early on a summer morning. Of course, he quickly agreed to this arrangement and was up and dressed in mere seconds.

We made it out the door in record time and breezed through his appointment. As we sat at McDonald's, spread out on yellow wrapping in front of each of us was a Sausage McMuffin with Egg and a hash brown snug in its white casing—a favorite treat for us both. We each took a bite of our hash browns first, and murmured a simultaneous "mmmmmmmmmm." We then set down our hash browns—still in their white casing to keep them warm—and got to the serious business of wolfing down our Sausage McMuffins with Egg, saving the remaining bites of hash brown for last.

In between bites of sandwich, Wil was telling me how funny the chef was on the movie "Princess and the Frog." He had me laughing, and looking back, I now believe it was a set-up. As I was thus distracted by his amusing story, he quickly reached across the table, grabbed my unsuspecting hash brown, the white casing falling off, and immediately took a huge bite. My hash brown! My McDonalds hash brown! The hash brown I was savoring for last. Do you know what he did next when I expressed my dismay? He laughed! Yes, he laughed, with his mouth full of my hash brown.

He chanted, "I stole Mom's hash brown!" and laughed again. He then picked up his own hash brown and finished eating it. I sat across the table from him, wide-mouthed in shock, my jaw about hitting the yellow wrapping in front of me with its lonely white casing lying upon it.

After breakfast on our drive back home, Wil continued his laughing and taunting chant, "I stole Mom's hash brown!" That is the end of my story. Now you know the truth. And I will never fall for another "Princess and the Frog" story again.

KNEE-DEEP IN PUBERTY

Stepping Up To The Bus

Wil got on the bus after school today. A simple statement. Yet backing that statement are hours of communications and miscommunications, collaborations and deliberations, facilitations and frustrations. Getting on the bus is the signature of a successful day. Not a perfect day, but a day where the stops were restarted again.

Winning doesn't always come with a trophy and cheering crowds. Winning the day may appear ordinary to most. But the steps of the victor are known to the one who has walked through the hours to arrive at their destination. The steps to the bus today were steps of victory.

Puberty

Wil's 13th birthday is in one month. His voice is getting deeper, he is growing by the day, and his appetite is hearty—as I type this, he is eating two ham and cheese sandwiches for breakfast. Wil is a dedicated Luke Bryan fan—he plays Luke's music daily and has made a point of memorizing every word of every one of his songs. (I have to remind Wil not to use country-favorite words like "beer" at school.) Wil's also feeling the urges that 13-year-old boys feel. He is affectionate by nature, but now that he's going through puberty, he is starting to hug too hard and too long.

We continue to work on setting boundaries, but that is a work in progress in these changing times for Wil. It's been quite a challenge. When it gets to a point that I need to separate Wil from his prolonged hugs, he feels sad, hurt, and upset. He'll flee the scene, which then becomes a safety issue. I am entering a new era with Wil that I need an education in.

I found a few helpful podcasts during my searches on the web. I've also talked to friends in our Down syndrome support group who also have children going through puberty. What I've discovered is this: there is no one concrete answer. As is the case in any transitionary time with our children, what works one day may very well not work the next.

The fact that I am in a constant state of learning and finding ways to be adaptable to the changes with Wil is nothing new. In discussing puberty with Katherine and Elizabeth, we read through American Girl books together. We had open conversations. Katherine and Elizabeth also attended health education at school that covered the topic of puberty. When Wil's class had health education, I opted him out, as the covered topics would have further confused him. Though puberty is a very natural part of growing up, Wil's body is ahead of his comprehension. I found I was unprepared for how complicated discussing these changes with him would be.

When Wil was a baby, I had many questions about explaining Down syndrome to Katherine and Elizabeth. This was further complicated by the fact that Katherine and Elizabeth are only 20 months older than Wil. They were so young, and yet I didn't want them to overhear their brother had Down syndrome from someone else and feel confused or hurt. I wanted them to understand as many facts as they were capable of at that time. But how to do that at their age? Whenever I tried to give them an explanation, it went right over their heads. I searched the web for answers. I listened to podcasts. I talked to friends in our Down syndrome support group. It was clear that what worked for one person did not always work for another. I bought the book called *We'll Paint the Octopus Red,* about a girl whose younger sibling was born with Down syndrome. The book is easy to read and designed to be understood by younger children. I read it to Katherine and Elizabeth multiple times. *We'll Paint the Octopus Red* is well-written and I recommend it to families to this day. Even though Katherine and Elizabeth enjoyed me reading this book to them, they never made the Down syndrome connection with their brother. They saw Wil as Wil— he did what he did and there was no reason to question why.

Then one summer day, shortly after Katherine and Elizabeth had completed Kindergarten, a key question came up. We were walking across the parking lot at Wil's preschool.

Elizabeth asked, "Mom, why is Wil in school now? I didn't have school the summer before Kindergarten."

I explained Wil needed extra help to complete certain tasks in school, and that was why he needed more school in the summer, too. That answer satisfied her—after my short explanation, she had already moved on to another topic. As much planning and questioning as I had done, the time had arrived on its own. Elizabeth had reached a stage where she was able to compare her progress with Wil's. At that point, she began to see there were differences between his schooling and hers. I may never know if the reading or explaining I did before her question that day had sunk in on some level. But I did make one important realization: No matter how prepared I am, certain experiences must arrive on their own time, in their own way. Certainly, my preparation helped when the time did come, but how and when it happened was beyond my control.

I am now reading books about puberty to Wil. He listens, but I'm not sure at this point if it is sinking in. Wil doesn't understand his changing emotions and changing body. Like most new subjects he learns, repetition is key. It will seem he doesn't understand for days or months on end, then one day— seemingly out of nowhere—it sinks in, and it feels as if I've just won the lottery. Right now, I'm taking lots of deep breaths, doing my best to be prepared, and letting time unfold as it will along the way.

During one of our reading sessions about puberty, I showed Wil a picture showing behavior that is acceptable in the privacy of his room as opposed to behavior that is acceptable in public. Wil looked at the picture in the book, gave it some thought, then looked up at me and said, "Ugh, Mom!" We both started laughing. Leave it up to Wil to sum up this whole puberty thing in two words.

How To Lift An Elephant

There is an analogy that no one can walk up to a grown elephant and have the strength to pick him up. However, if you begin by lifting the elephant in its infancy, and lift him each day, you will grow stronger as the elephant grows. One day you will find yourself with the strength to lift a grown elephant.

In these last few weeks, I feel not as if I've been lifting an infant elephant; rather that the infant elephant decided to sit down right on my stomach. I felt the slight shift of his infant weight, carrying on as usual. Then, day-by-day, his weight became perceptively heavier. Soon, I was dragging around and wondering how he got so big so fast.

Wil has been having some trouble at school. He started the school year like a rock star—popping out of bed, going to all of his classes, and taking the bus home. Katherine and Elizabeth were cranking out their first year of high school and I was able to coach more fitness classes at my place of work with the extra time Wil taking the bus home afforded me.

Then signs of stubbornness from Wil at school started to creep in. Wil would go through his day, with a few halts, but with the ability to overcome these few setbacks and still take the bus home. He'd arrive on our back porch step telling me all about his day, proud of his achievements. Then, he began to refuse certain lessons. One day it was reading, another day it was math—or he would flat out refuse to go into a classroom. There seemed to be no rhyme or reason. He'd put his foot down and it just wasn't going to happen. Wil would sit in the stairwell at school and refuse to move. I would be called to come and pick him up. I'd coax him off the stairwell. Sometimes he'd go willingly, other days it could take a good twenty minutes.

I'd go to work with knots in my stomach. What kind of day would it be? Would he have a few bumps or would today be full of refusal to work? Would I get a call to pick him up because he refused the bus? How would I pick him up if I was in the middle of coaching a class?

I make sure our mornings at home are upbeat so Wil begins his day with a strong start. Some mornings he wakes up agreeable and without effort. But as his obstinacy grew at school, he was refusing to get out of bed. He wasn't able to communicate to me fully why he was refusing to work. So while his teachers and I figured it all out, the mornings involved lots and lots of hugs, lots and lots of coaxing, and lots and lots of prompting and encouraging. These mornings also required lots and lots of patience from me. The elephant continued to grow and I was feeling his heavy weight. Not knowing how Wil's day would go—and not understanding what was triggering his behavior—was incredibly frustrating for Wil, for me, and for his teachers.

Wil has had challenging days before, but these behaviors, which I believe are due to his budding puberty mixed with a new school, are unfamiliar territory. We will figure it out, but in the process, not understanding what is upsetting Wil day after day continues to feed the elephant. Recently, I read this quote by David Steindl-Rast: "It is not joy that makes us grateful, it is gratitude that makes us joyful." I believe that to be true. I could paint a joyful rainbow on this ever-growing elephant and say, "Look how lovely he is! Oh how joyful!" And still, the now multi-hued elephant would not stop growing. His weight would still bear down on my joyful heart.

Many others carry elephants heavier than I do. I also carry full confidence we will get through this transition phase smarter and stronger for it. But sometimes it's plain cathartic to yell out the simple truth: "Dammit this is hard!" But this is where the gratitude comes in: When you are going along with your daily life, feeling the heavy weight holding you down, and poof! A spontaneous experience full of gratitude happens—an experience completely unrelated to your current issue at hand, that seems to place a wedge directly under the weight of the elephant to help lighten your load:

> I pulled my car into the post office parking lot and then opened the hatchback of my car. The back of my car was lined with crates loaded full of thank you letters and packages for our Buddy Walk sponsors and participants. (The Buddy Walk is an annual event to raise awareness and funds for individuals with Down syndrome.) The number of crates was more than I could carry into the post office in one load. A man with a Vietnam Veterans baseball cap walked over to me, surveyed the situation, and asked, "Do you want a little help?"
>
> "Yes, thank you." I said.
>
> "I'm retired, so I have the time. But in return," he said as he eyed all of the mailings, "you have to let me get in line in front of you."
>
> "You have a deal," I replied. After he helped me carry all of the packages in and we set them on a table, I got in line—of course, with him in front of me. I was in line long enough to overhear multiple conversations. A woman was sending a package to her granddaughter. She couldn't wait to see her next month. Another woman who took in a sickly dog that lived 15 years was mailing photos to the place she bought him from.

After my post office experience, I drove home with both my car and my heart feeling lighter from the multiple displays of kindness. Wil refused the bus that day, so I drove directly from the post office to pick him up at school. Wil loves music, so once in the car, he picked up my phone and pulled up Amazon Music. He found his favorite country singer, Luke Bryan, and chose the song, "Rain is a Good Thing." Even after a day of struggle, Wil let it all go as he sang along with Luke at the top of his lungs. Then, looking out the window, seeing the snow on the ground, he changed the word "rain" to "snow." He sang, "Where I come from, snow is a good thiiiiiiing! Oh yeah!"

Even though I was more than ready for the fresh start of spring, I rolled down the windows, and we both sang at the top of our lungs, the cold, fresh air on our faces, "Snow is a good thiiiiiiing!"

There is strength is gratitude. And joy can be found in that strength. Strength to lift the elephant no matter the weather— be it rain, snow, or sunshine.

Where Is The Fast-Forward Button?

I meditate… 10 minutes a day… with Headspace. I get to choose when and where I meditate. My chosen 10 minutes of living in the present is bliss. It is very Zen.

But being put in the present moment when it's not my chosen 10 minutes? Is there a fast-forward button on this present moment thing?

Last night Matt and I both got home about 7pm. Wil had two sheets of homework. Just one sheet, depending on his mood, can take either hours or minutes. Currently, Wil is congested. So he's tired. Hours, rather than minutes, was the likely scenario. We usually start homework about 4:30 so Wil can take multiple breaks, if needed. Knowing I'd be home later, I asked Katherine and Elizabeth to work on one of the sheets with him, giving him breaks, and I'd complete the rest with him when I got home. Katherine and Elizabeth are very good at doing homework with Wil, and he enjoys his big sisters' help. But even they could only elicit answers to 3 of the 25 questions from Wil. In the end, pulling out all the silliness, encouragement, and creativity we could muster, 7 questions were answered—the other sheet remained completely blank. Wil went to bed and immediately fell asleep. I did the same. It was exhausting for all of us.

You can't press the fast-forward button on Wil. The minute he senses force, he responds with like force. Taking breaks is a necessity. A brief break can save hours. He requires encouragement. Silliness always wins. Creativity is a must. Some days are a breeze, and other days, like last night, are stumpers.

On school mornings, I wake Wil up knowing it will take him 10-30 minutes to get out of bed. He requires a hug first. Then another hug. And another. And another. Then tickles and lots of giggles. Then we decide on what's for breakfast. Eating breakfast is a hot topic. He loves to eat, and it's usually leftovers from dinner or a sandwich. He's not into cereal. After breakfast, brushing his teeth is another process. He is a sensory kid, and this too requires patience, silliness, and creativity. Some days, brushing his teeth is left until after school because of the time it can take.

All of these moments with Wil require me to be present. Any attempt to press the fast-forward button and it's like hitting rewind. Though I can predict these times with a fair amount of accuracy, they are not my chosen times to be in the present moment.

At this point in my life, I don't believe that being in the present moment is always filled with bliss. That is, if it's not at a time of our choosing. When I really want to press the fast-forward button on Wil, but know I cannot, I have to find my silliness. I have to find my creativity. I have to find another well of patience. Some days I do better than others. When I reach a point of losing my cool, I get more creative. I get sillier. And my well deepens even more. So while the present moment is not always what I'd call bliss, I'm still deeply grateful for my growth in it.

Maybe that is the lesson of the present moment: it's not always about bliss and being. Maybe the present moment is meant to be about growth and gratitude. At least that is the theory I'm going with right now. And I've got about a million morning hugs to back that theory up.

Catching Flies

This morning when I went into Wil's room to wake him up, he was lying face up, head tilted slightly back, and mouth wide open. Catching flies, as my mom used to say.

I decided to let him keep up his fly-catching another 10 minutes. We could spare that time and it would do him good. For most of us, sleep is central to having a successful day. In Wil, lack of sleep is quite noticeable. If his 8:30pm bedtime is extended to 9pm, the slight half-hour change can mean the difference between a productive day and a drag-your-feet day.

When I did wake Wil up, he was good-natured, but slow to move. He was full of hugs, good mornings, and giggles. I teased him that if he didn't get out of bed, I would eat him up for breakfast. Katherine hollered from the other room, "No Mom, I'm eating Wil for breakfast!"

"Hey, I called Wil for breakfast first, Katherine!" I hollered back.

"Nope, he's mine, Mom, and I'm hungry!" Katherine said walking toward Wil's room.

"Hey! Stop it! I'm not a food!" Wil bolted upright in bed.

"Aha, gotcha moving," I thought silently. I hug-lifted Wil out of bed and got him to his dresser. He's very particular about what he wears, so I left him to his own devices to get dressed.

Wil emerged a few minutes later, fully dressed. "Look at me, Mom!" He had on a turquoise shirt and khaki-colored pants. Wil has a knack for making just about anything fun. Every single morning, he comes out thrilled with his outfit choice.

"Looking sharp, Wil—I have your breakfast," I said.

"Thanks Mom," Wil replied.

"Wil, you just make everything fun," I said.

Living with Wil, a lot of things I used to fret over or get upset about just don't matter like they used to. I would just be plain exhausted all the time. I can't afford to have a bad day with Wil—if I do, it means *he* will have a bad day, and that swings right back to me. It's not a good cycle.

I need to be patient Every. Single. Day. Not because I'm a patient person. Not because I have been bestowed some special gift. I can't just expect Wil to do something because "I told you so." I also have to rely on a lot of people for Wil's success. Just this morning, I sat at a table at the school for a review of Wil's behavior plan, thanking my lucky stars Wil has those people by his side. Because you get the team you get in your school. You don't have much choice in the matter—you have to make it work with the team you have or change schools.

On a daily basis, I must be patient when I feel I have no patience left. On a daily basis, I must let certain expectations go and allow them to unfold in their own time. And for this, on a daily basis, I'm more able to deeply celebrate Wil proudly walking out of his room in whatever clothing combination he has created.

I celebrate Wil making a choice to take on his day after much patient nudging and creativity has been put in place. I celebrate the dexterity Wil now has to get dressed on his own (he still needs help on small buttons, so thank you Old Navy for having pull-up pants in his size). I celebrate Wil taking ownership of his accomplishments and personal choices.

When you are introduced to the ability to celebrate the workings behind what most people take for granted, like putting on a turquoise shirt and khakis, you have been granted the ability to create happiness out of just about anything. Having that ability is the catch of a lifetime.

Morning Wash

This morning it took a full-on 30 minutes to rouse Wil out of bed. This is how it went:

"Wil, time to get up."

"Hi, Mom."

"Good morning, Wil."

"Good night, Mom." He giggled and pulled the covers over his head.

"No, it's good morning Wil," I said as I pulled the covers back down.

"Good night, Mom." He giggled and pulled the covers back over his head.

"Good morning, Wil." I pulled the covers down. I gave him a hug while I lifted him up. "Do you want me to help you get dressed?"

"No, I do it."

"Ok, it's time to get dressed then. I'll go make you breakfast."

"Ok, Mom." Then he plopped back down and pulled the covers over his head.

"Wil, you have to get up now. Chop chop!" I clapped my hands and he laughed.

"Oh, Mom. You are silly." I did fast little claps near his face. He grabbed my hands, pulled me down, and gave me a hug.

"You are sillier," I said, hugging him back. I lifted him up to a seated position. "Ok, let's go. So you don't have a rushed breakfast."

"Ok, Mom."

"Here, I'll get your underwear out for you, then you pick out your pants and shirt." I set his underwear down on the bed next to him and headed to the doorway. I turned around to see him sitting there watching me. I knew he would lie right back down when I left.

"Wil, please, let's go. You won't have time for breakfast if you keep up this pace."

"Ok, ok, ok," He said. Convinced he would truly get up this time, I left the room and came back a few minutes later to check on him.

"Look, Mom, I put my underwear on." Wil was standing in the middle of his room, his pajama bottoms and top still on, but he had his fresh pair of underwear pulled up over his pajama bottoms. I knew laughing would slow things down even more, but I couldn't help it. I started cracking up, then he started cracking up as he began dancing around the room in his "over-underwear."

"Wil, you are just too cute. That is funny. Ok, I'm sorry to end the party, but we are down to the wire here. Pretty please, let's get dressed. With your underwear under your clothes."

He danced around some more, then said, "Ok, Mom, go." That meant he wanted privacy to get dressed.

Finally, he walked into the kitchen. He had on pants and a hoodie sweatshirt, with his underwear under. He sat down at the kitchen table and got right to business eating his breakfast. No need for convincing or coaxing in that department.

Some of our minutes are under, some of our minutes are over, but it all evens out in the wash.

Happy Happy Joy Joy

Wil has had a tough few days. Some days I can identify the triggers for these challenging days, and some days I cannot. On this day, I knew what the trigger was. In an unusual set of circumstances, I worked late the previous night and early that morning. This means I did not put Wil to bed or wake him up the next morning. There are two mornings a week Katherine and Elizabeth wake Wil up and help him get ready for school. I arrive home just in time to take them all to school. Those mornings typically go fine, but that is when I've been home to put Wil to bed the night before.

I prepared Wil by telling him that I would not be home that evening or the next morning. I explained that I'd come in his room when I got home from work to give him a hug that evening, and that Katherine and Elizabeth would be there in the morning. He seemed to be agreeable to the situation when I talked to him. However, when I returned from work in the morning, it was clear things were not going well. He was disagreeable to most suggestions, went on to have a challenging day at school, and refused to take the bus home.

The previous day at school was also challenging. I'm not sure what the triggers were that day, but it was what it was. To prevent a third challenging day in a row, I woke Wil up 10 minutes early the following morning. I always lie down with him in the morning (other than the mornings his sisters wake him up) and we take about 10 minutes to laugh and giggle while he asks for lots of hugs. Waking him up 10 minutes early meant we got 20 minutes of laughs, giggles, and hugs, and he got out of bed singing, "Happy, Happy, Joy, Joy, Happy, Happy, Joy!" all morning.

For breakfast that morning, Wil ate a turkey burger (he's a dinner-for-breakfast kind of guy). When I heated up some egg casserole that we had made the night before for myself, he stole that from me and ate it too. I knew he was in for a good day.

The night before, I hadn't been sure if he would have a turnaround. We had multiple stops and starts with his homework. He was humming along, writing out the answers to all of the questions, until he reached the word, "P-r-e-s-i-d-e-n-t." He wrote a "t" instead of "d." "Oh, Wil, hold on, that's supposed to be a d," I said. "Presi DDDent."

"No, t. Presitent."

"It can sound like a "t" but it's a 'd.' Presi DDDent."

He said, "No, t." He put his pencil down and crossed his arms. Fortunately, there was time to burn in the evening and we only had a few questions left to answer.

"Hey Wil," I said, "how about we take a break. You've done an amazing job getting through this. Let's finish after dinner."

"Ok, Mom." I never quite know how "after dinner" will go. So after dinner I asked, "Wil, how about we finish those last few questions?"

"Ok, Mom!" he said. I breathed a sigh of relief. Wil agreed to the "d" this time around and completed the remainder of his questions. "Ok," I said, "pajama time and then some free time before bed."

"Ok, Mom!"

Now it was my turn to sing, "Happy, Happy, Joy, Joy, Happy, Happy, Joy!"

Shake A Tailfeather

Driving home from work this morning, I received a call from Katherine.

"Mom, Wil is in the shower and he won't get out. We have to leave for school in 15 minutes."

"Ok," I said, "see if you can urge him out of the shower. If not, keep getting yourself ready and I'll be home in five minutes. Has Wil eaten yet?"

"No."

"Ok, what does he want for breakfast?"

"Sandwiches."

"Ok good, thanks. I can make those quickly. See you soon, Katherine."

This is no new scenario. Some mornings, Wil hops out of bed ready to go, and other mornings he requires more time. We all have those kinds of mornings for whatever reason. The challenging part is, where we all understand the need for urgency, Wil could care less about it. Any rushing sets you 10 steps back.

Not too long ago, Wil would not get out of bed. Would not— no, no, no. Even with the most patience, he was stuck in a funk. He was moving so slow that there was no way the three of them wouldn't be late for school. I convinced Wil to at least get in the car so I could take his sisters to school on time—it wasn't fair for them to be late—and that the two of us would go back and finish getting ready. Even with that extra time, he still had a challenging day. Funky moods can be hard to break for all of us. Consider having communication barriers where you are unable to express in words how you are feeling and it makes it all the more frustrating.

When these challenging mornings are happening, there are typically three key questions I try to answer: Is he staying in the shower out of independence? Is it an act of defiance? Or is he simply enjoying the shower and not ready to get out? If it's about independence, that's an easy one. Wil is generally in good spirits and wants to determine his shower time like most teens. With some pleasant urging, he's typically willing to get out of the shower and dressed for school. But if he's rushed, this situation can easily move into the second question. If he's staying in the shower as an act of defiance, then there is no question he will be late for school. His defiance means there is something brewing under the surface and I need to find a way to help him get through it. This takes time. Any amount of rushing and his heels will find a way to dig into the slippery shower floor until he is good and ready to get out. Giving him time and allowing him to regroup his emotions is the most effective way to work through these situations. Question #3 is my favorite. Don't we all like to linger in the shower a little longer?

When I arrived home, sure enough, Wil was still in the shower. I pulled back the shower curtain.

"Hi, Mommy! Watch this." Wil did a pantomime dive down to the base of the tub and started to pretend to swim. I breathed a sigh of relief. There were no signs of defiance. He was clearly just enjoying his time in the shower.

"That's really good you little fish, " I said. "Hey, it's time to get to school. If we move fast enough, you'll still have time to eat one of your two sandwiches. You can take the other one with you." (Wil loves to take his unfinished breakfast into school.)

"Ok," he said. I breathed another sigh of relief at his immediate agreement. Wil stepped out of the shower, picked up his towel, held it in front of him, and shook his bare little tail feather in a dance. I wrapped the towel around him and he ran off, still dripping water, to his bedroom.

When I followed him into his bedroom, I saw he had already picked out his clothes. His shirt, pants, and underwear were all neatly stacked on his bed. I was thankful to see this sign of independence. We had five minutes left. I slapped together his sandwiches and he ate one while I put on and tied his shoes. I put the other sandwich in a Tupperware dish for him to carry into school.

"Here, Wil. This has your sandwich in it that you can take to school." I said.

"Ok, thank you," he replied.

Other than a prolonged shower, Wil was clearly looking forward to his day at school. With all that had transpired, we left the house only three minutes later than usual and the kids arrived at school on time. I know all the different ways these types of mornings can go; when I pulled back the shower curtain this morning, I did not know what I was going to get. Having experienced all the different directions it could have gone, I chalk this morning up as a major success. We *all* shook a tail feather, and arrived at school with virtual gold medals hanging around our necks.

From Monday To Friday in 60 Minutes

When I woke Wil up, he was very sluggish.

"Hey, buddy, time to wake up," I said. I sat on the edge of his bed and tickled him lightly under his chin.

"Hmmph!" Wil turned his face into his pillow and commenced fake snoring.

"Oh Wil, I almost forgot. It's your favorite day of the week today. It's Monday. Happy Monday, Will!" Wil turned his head from his pillow, opened his clenched eyes, and looked up at me.

"Ugh, Mom. It's Friday."

"Hmmm, I'm pretty sure it's Monday today. Let's go Monday!"

"Mom," he bolted upright in bed, "it's Friday."

"Ok, I guess it's Friday. Ho-hum. How boring. The end of a week of school. I think the beginning is much more fun. Too bad it's not Monday. Time to get dressed now."

"Oh, Moooooom. Hugs now."

"Yes, we can't forget our hugs," I said, and hugged him. "Ok, let's get up and dressed and ready for our Monday."

"Oh, Moooooom. Ok, I'll get dressed. Go Friday!"

Later that morning as I was driving all three kids to school, Elizabeth said, "So Wil, what's for lunch on Mondays?"

"It's FRIDAY!" Wil replied.

"Oh, it is? Phew, I thought it was Monday," Elizabeth said. Then as they all exited the car at school, Elizabeth said to me, "Have a great Monday, Mom!"

"You too, Elizabeth!"

"Sheesh, you guys. It's FRIDAY! Let's go Friday!" Wil laughed and took off running to the school.

A sluggish start can easily extend itself into a very challenging day at school for Wil. Silliness is the kryptonite to his sluggishness—it doesn't always work, but it's always worth a try (and the bonus is the silly start added fun for all of us). Let's go Friday!

Friday, Friday, Friday!

I have not hidden the challenges of experiencing puberty with Wil. Though I could have guessed what puberty with Wil would look like, there are certain things you simply need to experience to be fully in the know.

I talked to Wil's teacher consultant for ideas on working with his new behaviors associated with puberty. His teacher consultant has worked with multiple children with varying abilities. When I approached her, the first thing she did was ask me questions. She didn't make assumptions based on Wil having Down syndrome. Though she is very experienced in working with kids with Down syndrome, it was important for her to know and understand Wil as the individual he is.

The other morning, Wil was being extremely willful. It took him a full 30 minutes to get out of bed and ready for school. The pattern continued throughout the day and into the evening. Wil didn't want to go to Katherine's CrossFit class that night, but Elizabeth was at basketball and Matt was out of town, so going to CrossFit was his only choice, as he is not able to stay home alone at this point. Katherine and I finally convinced Wil to go to her class, with the promise of a stop at Biggby Coffee for a cup of hot chocolate with sprinkles. I took a deep breath when we finally succeeded in getting him into the car.

We played music on the drive to CrossFit and all seemed to be going well. After dropping Katherine off, Wil and I headed to Biggby Coffee. I ordered his hot chocolate and he drank most of it. We shared a conversation, with a few pauses and prompting. When it was time to pick up Katherine at CrossFit, he refused to leave Biggby Coffee. Again, with lots of convincing, I finally got him out of his chair and into the car.

When we arrived home, he had some time to watch television and then go to bed. He refused to go to bed. Thankfully, we didn't have anywhere to go, so I walked him to his bedroom and told him he could stay in there until he was ready to put on his pajamas. This is usually a successful tactic, as it gives him time to unwind and feel back in control of his situation. It can take anywhere from 15 minutes to an hour. It took an hour.

By the time I got Wil into bed, I was exhausted from the constant negotiations of the day. Instead of going to bed myself, I felt the need to unwind and feel back in control of my situation too. I sat down and read a book until I felt calmed down, then I went to bed. I fell asleep the second I laid down.

When Matt returned to town, I told him about this experience. I explained how Wil's behavior had been challenging the entire day. I had tried to get Wil to communicate, but he was being obstinate with anything I did.

"Hmm, sounds like a teenager to me," Matt said.

The next week the kids would have Friday and Monday off school in observance of President's Day. The Thursday morning preceding the holiday weekend, Wil popped out of bed singing, "Friday, Friday, Friday!"

"Wil, it's Thursday," I said.

"No, it's Friday, Friday, Friday!" he continued singing.

"Huh, you know what? You are right. In school days, this is your Friday. Hooray Friday, Friday, Friday!"

He went on to have a very productive day at school. However, the Tuesday after the holiday was not so celebratory. Having had the preceding Friday and Monday off school, Wil was well out of his routine. He refused to get on the bus after school on Tuesday, and even escaped outside for a brief period. His teacher was on it, though, and rallied him back in. When I entered the school office to pick him up, he was fairly cheerful—no doubt due to his brush with fresh air and freedom.

"Wil, you were all excited to ride the bus home when I dropped you off for school this morning. What happened?"

"Mondays are hard, Mom," he said. I almost said it was Tuesday, then caught myself. In school days, it was his Monday. I also couldn't argue that Mondays can be hard.

Refusing the bus ride home on Mondays is more the rule than the exception. If I were to graph Wil's week, it would represent an upward slope. As the week progresses, Wil falls into the groove of a routine. Though no day is smooth sailing, his days progressively become more productive. Wil earns stars for completing work in each of his classes. He earned a mere 4 stars that Tuesday, but doubled his count by Thursday. On Friday he promised to repeat an 8-star day. And he did. Hooray for Friday, Friday, Friday!

When Wil was a baby, I read multiple books about Down syndrome. Books about babies with Down syndrome all the way through books about teenagers and young adults with Down syndrome. I wanted to put myself in the know. There were way too many unknowns when I learned of Wil's diagnosis. Reading books helped put me in the know—or so I thought. Though reading was extremely helpful, I was still only partially in the know. Reading is one thing. Experiencing is another.

Wil is a teenager and he also has Down syndrome. Sometimes those two ingredients are mutually exclusive, and sometimes they mix. Wil has tough Mondays and cheers on his Fridays, Fridays, Fridays! Wil has 4-star days and 8-star days. Wil's week goes in an upward curve quite predictably, but what happens along that curve is anyone's guess.

The only advice I can offer up to this point is to keep your head up, always work toward an upward curve, and ask lots of questions. Each day is its own, with its own set of rules— sometimes our Mondays are our Tuesdays. Be wary of those who claim to know the answers—only those who ask questions truly seek the answers. You don't know what you don't know until you do know. Once you do know, you realize the only constant is change. And, most of all, never forget to celebrate Friday, Friday, Friday! (Even when it falls on a Thursday.)

Play, Pray, And Don't Say Beer At School

I ran into Wil's bedroom and started cheering, "It's Friday, it's Friday, it's Friday!"

He rolled over, giggled, and pulled the covers over his head. I put my hands on his back and pushed down, then released; pushed down, released—over and again, bouncing him on his bed, singing, "It's Friday, it's Friday, it's Friday!"

He laughed, craned his head up to look at me, and said, "Ok, ok, ok, Mom, just calm down."

"I will if you get out of bed."

Still lying on his stomach, he scrunched his body up, with his tushy sticking up in the air. I gave it a swat and said, "Get your little booty out of bed."

"Look Mom, I'm an inch worm," he replied as he wiggled on the bed.

"You are a very cute inch worm. And you are going to be a late inch worm if you don't get dressed soon."

"Ok, Mom, hugs." He sat up and reached out for a hug. As I leaned in to give him one, he bear-hugged me. I lifted him up and out of bed. He curled up his legs so his feet wouldn't touch the floor. I felt my neck and back cinch up, and leaned him back over the bed.

"Wil, you are not little anymore. You can hurt Mommy doing that. Ok, up and at 'em!"

"Huuuuugs." I hugged him again, then he laid back down in bed.

"Wil, up, up, up!"

"Oh, Mom, too much energy. Hugs." I hugged him again, and pulled him up.

"Ok, Mom, go."

"You promise to get dressed if I go?"

"Ugh, yes, Mooooom." From a playful inchworm to an irritated teenager in seconds.

We decided what he wanted for breakfast—"Mac 'n' cheese?" "No." "Sandwich?" "No." "Eggs?" "No." "Oatmeal?" "Yuck, Mooooom." "Ok, hot sandwich?" <pause> "Yes, and tomato soup."

As I left Wil's bedroom to make his breakfast, I pulled the door almost shut so I could peek through the crack to make sure he was getting dressed. After putting the sandwiches on the stove, I quietly walked up to his bedroom and peeked in. He was talking to himself about his outfit. He always puts his pants on first, then his shirt. When I help him get dressed after his swim lesson, and I forget this rule, he looks at me like I'm a crazy person. He'll tell me very matter-of-factly, "Pants first, Mom, then shirt."

Wil always has a theme in mind when he gets dressed. On Monday that week, he emerged from his room, threw his hands up in the air, and proclaimed, "Gray Power!" He had on a gray hooded sweatshirt with gray pants. He also happened to match the winter sky that day. I thought, that's one way to make the most out of a gray day. Especially on a Monday. Unfortunately, even though that day started on a high, it ended on a low. His teachers and I weren't sure of the triggers to his behaviors, but he refused to work in his afternoon classes. I picked him up after school, as he also refused to take the bus home.

He walked out of his room this morning with a Luke Bryan concert T-shirt his Aunt Carrie bought him. "Look at me, Mom." (Last night watching Jeopardy, I said to Wil, "if they had Luke Bryan as a category, you would win." "Really, what?" he asked and ran up to the television, mistaking my comment for Jeopardy having a real-time Luke Bryan category. He yelled out, "Kill the Lights!" "Here's to the Farmer!" "Strip it Down!" "M-O-V-E!" "Drink a Beer," then, under his breath, "No, don't say that at school. Don't say beer at school.")

Wil sat down to eat the breakfast I made him—two warm ham, cheese, and spinach sandwiches on whole wheat buns and a bowl of tomato soup heated to a lukewarm temperature (he doesn't like anything hot).

"Which shoes do you want today, Wil? Black or brown?" The black shoes are his tennis shoes and the brown are somewhat dressier. Today he chose brown, even though he wore sweatpants with his Luke Bryan shirt.

When it was time to go, he still had half of one of the sandwiches and some soup left. Occasionally this happens—I believe on purpose—because he wants to bring some of his breakfast to school. I put his sandwich in a baggie with a plastic spoon and poured the remainder of the soup into a thermos.

He pulled on his backpack, grabbed his baggie and thermos, and we were off. He sang Luke Bryan songs the entire way to school. (When I'm driving by myself, I can't listen to a Luke Bryan song—it's lackluster without Wil's backup.)

When I brought the car to a stop in front of the school, Wil bolted out with a quick, "Bye, Mom," and in his low muscle tone way, ran without much bend in his knees, moving slightly side to side, his backpack bouncing on his back, baggie and thermos in hand. I sent up a prayer for his good spirits to continue.

Every day is a process, with or without a playful start. It's fun when kids are younger, but now Wil is 13. In many ways, I'm thankful for his continued youthful spirit, and in other ways the process gets tiring after so many years. His independence is growing in leaps and bounds, yet still, he requires lots of encouragement to get on with his day and with extracurricular activities. I've tried to rush him, and it backfires each time. In fact, a little reverse psychology can go a long way. I used to say, "Quick like a bunny!" but now I say, "Slow as a tortoise." He'll start slow, find it to be funny, then get on to the activity.

While a playful start doesn't guarantee a good day, my own personal calculations show a sharp rise in success when it happens. So I play the numbers, inch by inch, each and every day. Once he bolts out the car door, in the mix with many other kids and experiences, it's anyone's guess as to what may trigger him to turn the day upside down or flip it back around and land right side up. That's when a good team at school and prayers come in handy.

> *Give us this day our daily hot sandwich and tomato soup, as we start our day in play, may we keep our day right side up, and remember not to say "beer" at school. Amen.*

Timberlake Vs Timbuktu

Wil had a quiz to study for. We decided together that he would study while Katherine was at CrossFit. If Wil comes along to CrossFit for a task such as studying, we typically go to Biggby Coffee and he gets a hot chocolate with sprinkles. After a few sips, some silliness, and conversation, we get down to the business at hand. Last night he said no to Biggby.

"Where do you want to go?"

"Hmmm, don't know."

"How about McDonalds. You can get a chocolate shake, then we'll study for your quiz."

"Ok."

When we arrived at McDonalds, we had an hour until we needed to be back to pick up Katherine. Wil made a quick scan of the play area. It was empty.

He tugged on my arm. "Mom, in there."

"Ok, let's order your shake first." We walked up to the kiosk. He squinted.

"Put on your glasses, Wil."

"No."

"Here, just try." I handed his glasses to him.

"Hey, I can see it."

"Um, yeah silly. That's why we like you to wear your glasses. You can see so much better." He wears glasses for reading and occupational therapy—other than that, he has no interest in them.

Wil made his chocolate shake order through the kiosk, reading every word proudly out loud.

"Great job, Wil."

After the order was complete, he pulled off his glasses and headed toward the play structure, his arm extended back to me with the glasses.

After playing in the play structure with lots of "look at me's," two other young boys entered. The increased noise level was enough for Wil and he made a quick exit. I followed him with his shake. He picked a table in the main area and we took a seat.

"Here are your glasses Wil. Let's do a little studying now."

The subject of the quiz was the Empire of Ghana. His teacher had condensed the lesson for him. After we got through the definition of Mali, the Niger River, and Mansa Musa, I asked him, "What was the major trading city when Mali was at the height of its power?"

"Timberlake!"

"Wil, Justin Timberlake is a singer. He's the voice of Branch in Trolls."

"I see your true colors shining through, I see your true colors and that's why I love you…"

"You love Trolls."

"You?"

"Yes, I love Trolls too, Wil. And Justin Timberlake is a really good singer and dancer. But the answer isn't Timberlake. Let's try again. What's the major trading city?"

"Timberlake!"

"Wil."

"Timberlake!"

"Wil, come on."

"Timberlake!"

"Ok, it's Timbuktu. Can you at least say Timbuktu for me?"

"Timberlake!"

"You are so silly. Do you want to watch a Timberlake video?"

"Yes, Can't Stop the Feeling."

We watched "Can't Stop the Feeling" and "True Colors." Then we got back to the quiz. I jumped ahead to the next definitions and we got through those fairly smoothly, with the exception of mosque. He looked hard at the word and came up with "message."

"Wil, good try, it's mosque."

"MosKE."

"That's right, say it again."

"Message."

"Honey, you just had it right. Mosque. Say it again. Mosque."

"MosKE."

"Good, again."

"MosKE."

"Good, ten times fast."

"MosKE, MosKE, MosKE, MosKE, Ugh, ok Mom."

"You got it."

Then we circled back to Timbuktu.

"Ok, Wil, what was the major trading city?"

"Timberlake!"

"Can you at least tell me you'll answer Timbuktu on the quiz?"

"Timberlake!"

Teamwork

Wil's team and I had a follow-up meeting on his behavior plan. Wil has had bumps in the road before, but this is the first time we've needed a behavior plan. The mix of hormones on the edge of being a 13-year-old and the growing communication and processing gaps between Wil and his typical peers has necessitated this development. Wil's resource room teacher, paraprofessional, teacher consultant, social worker, and speech therapist were all present at the behavior plan meeting. After the initial pleasantries, we got down to business.

We created the initial behavior plan about a month ago. This follow-up meeting was to discern what aspects of the plan were working, what areas required more detail, and any other parts of the plan that needed to be re-mapped or removed. I can't say exactly when, but at some point during the meeting, I was overwhelmed with the thought that we were all sitting around this table together, in this room, for Wil. Yes, it is a statement of the obvious. But if you really think about that fact in and of itself, it's powerful.

Surely, you can poke holes in any program or its processes. But I thought of my mom's friend's son. He is my age and has Down syndrome. There was no such team for him. There were no meetings or plans put in place. It's hard to believe that at one time, these rights for Wil did not exist. Wil's rights are protected under IDEA. IDEA was first known as the Education of Handicapped Children Act, but even that did not pass until 1975. That's really not so long ago. My mom's friend's son was born before this act passed. Bringing her son home from the hospital without institutionalizing him was a highly progressive choice at that time.

Most parents back then, upon learning their child had Down syndrome, were told their child would be a burden to the entire the family—their marriage would surely be strained, siblings would suffer, and the child would not be able to talk, read, or write—maybe not even walk. Their child would never leave home. Institutionalizing their child was surely the most humane choice for all involved. My mom's friend was a pioneer simply for the fact that she chose to take her child home to raise.

Laws like IDEA are powerful, but even so, those of us working within the guidelines of these laws are human, bringing with us our own emotions and interpretations. Two weeks prior to this follow-up meeting, I was not able to step back and appreciate the whole of Wil's team and the laws built by those before us. Wil's behaviors had escalated and I was receiving almost daily calls from the school. Getting Wil out of bed every morning was at least a half-hour process, and it was becoming a given that he would completely shut down every day at lunchtime. Whether Wil would get on the bus or not was the question of the day. The tension within me was building as this continued day-after-day-after-day. I knew Wil was hurting inside, and his team and I were not able to crack his code. To ask me to step back and appreciate the laws and team that protected him would have been beyond my emotional capabilities at that time.

Fortunately, I realized that I was at an emotional breaking point. I knew I was in a place where I could only see one step in front of me and I may be missing a lot of clues that someone from the outside looking in could see plainly. I called Wil's teacher consultant. She has known Wil since he was in preschool. She also sat in on his IEP (individualized education program) and initial behavior plan meeting. While she does not work with Wil on a day-to-day basis, she does have a vast knowledge of behaviors and how to work with them. When I called her, I told her where I was emotionally—that I could be missing critical pieces because I could not see outside of where I was. I asked if she could help give me a broader lens to look through. She immediately put me at ease, validated my concerns, and helped educate me in these new areas I was navigating with Wil. It was a turning point for me. She also called Wil's team, and the tides began to turn at school too.

Wil's behaviors began to fall in line with the plan. We have not struck gold, though it feels like it right now. There is no perfect plan. But there is a plan that works right now, and this is that plan. After living and learning through those challenging weeks, I am able to step back, even when I need to step forward. There is no real cracking of the code to certain behaviors. But there is always a new discovery to be found in the experience.

Sitting at the table with Wil's team for his behavior plan that morning, I was able to take in the whole and appreciate how we were able to work through the kinks to get where we are now. I was able to appreciate that Wil is getting out of bed easily in the mornings, taking the bus home, and not objecting to homework. What many take for granted, Wil, his team, and I take as victories. Wil did have a rough day the Monday after Thanksgiving break, and with the holidays coming up, the variances in schedule will likely cause more bumps in the road. I also know the full moon causes waves in behavior too, not just the tide. Wil's behavior plan will continue to be a work in progress.

Each day, month, and year I learn more. I learn more about the law and I learn more about human behavior— first and foremost, mine! I will always be Wil's first and biggest advocate until he can be that for himself. Then I will be standing tall right beside him when he needs me. That said, it also takes a village. I find myself in both awe of and thankful for the village that we have. Though we are all human, and we all have our own breaking points, we are together for one purpose—the success of Wil Taylor. This is a team of people who love him, people who support him, and people who want the very best for him. They believe in his future and in his potential. Not because a law says so, but because they care.

This team comes together for the success of one, and for that very purpose we as a team and as individuals stand stronger, raise the bar higher, and become wiser with each and every experience.

Yell It On The Mountaintop

Raising a child with special needs is no walk in the park. Behavior functions as communication, especially when verbal skills are delayed. You learn to anticipate certain behaviors. You learn to ask questions: What did that behavior mean? Was there a trigger today? Or was it something the night before? Or maybe it was just one of those days we all have, with no rhyme or reason.

Wil is not yet able to fully communicate to me his emotions and the details of his day. He was having a particularly hard time last week. His teachers and I were trying our best to understand the triggers to his behaviors. On one day, his resource room teacher texted me that the prospect of Wil getting on the bus that day did not look good. He was refusing to work all afternoon. A buildup of this behavior had me upset—I was ready to lay down some strict rules. But whatever you enforce will show up in a different behavior. I need to work to solve the puzzle of what he's trying to communicate.

When I arrived at school to pick Wil up, his resource room teacher had good news. Together, they had made a breakthrough. She asked Wil what he was going to do, and he yelled out loudly and proudly, "Talk!"

She repeated her question and he again yelled out loudly and proudly, "Talk!"

Wil and his teacher repeated this chant again and again, then fell apart laughing.

I laughed with them as my eyes welled with tears. My goodness, what a milestone! Wil's resource room teacher found a way to get through to Wil that day. Even yesterday, Wil may have not been ready for that chant. But by observing his behavior changes and asking lots of questions, mixed with a pinch of luck, Wil's teacher was able to meet Wil exactly where he was at exactly the right time.

No, raising a child with special needs is no walk in the park—it's more like a climb. A climb where you can't quite see the mountaintop above. You reach, you stumble, you reach and stumble again, wondering if you're getting anywhere. But with patience, perseverance, lots of questions, and a pinch of luck, one day—at just the right time—you find yourself at the mountaintop. You stand tall, take in the view, your eyes welling with happy tears. You firmly place a flag in that very spot and declare loudly and proudly from that mountaintop, "We've reached a milestone!"

STANDING TALL WITH
SIBLINGS AND FRIENDS

You Can't Get Tired

Katherine, Elizabeth, and I were talking about the Connect program at their school (a peer-to-peer program that connects students with special needs and typically-developing students). I mentioned that an acquaintance of theirs, who has a brother with autism, is involved with Connect.

"She has to be very valuable to the program," I said, "as she understands this life inside and out. I know you both would also be valuable to Connect, if you choose to participate next year. But I would also understand if you didn't want to, too. You live this life every day. Maybe you would grow tired of it."

"Mom," Elizabeth said, "when you live it every day, you can't grow tired of it. You just can't do that."

"You are wise beyond your years, Elizabeth."

Connect

Many schools have a peer-to-peer program in the middle and/or high schools. These programs are where a typically developing student is linked with a student with special needs. At our school, this program is called Connect. Wil, who is in 7th grade, has been linked with two high school students, Nathan and Libbey.

Nathan and Libbey visit Wil during his Independent Life Skills time in the resource room. They also work with him on projects, crafts, and cooking—Wil especially enjoys cooking with Nathan and Libbey. It's been an enriching experience for Wil to work with his Connect friends and, I believe, for his Connect friends to work with him. On days when Wil is feeling unmotivated, his teachers will remind him he is seeing Nathan and Libbey, and on most days, that will perk him up.

Middle school is an interesting time for most students. Their bodies are changing, their hormones are firing, and they're seeking their independence. Wil is no different. His assertion for independence has him taking a few liberties with Nathan and Libbey. He may pick up one of their spoons and throw it on the floor, or give them a hug then mess up their hair. He's pushing the boundaries, and also looking for attention. If he were a typical student throwing a friend's spoon on the floor, or messing their hair, he'd get a "Hey, what did you do that for?" However, kids with special needs tend to get some extra latitude. Wil may get a laugh, rather than a reprimand. Or his behavior will go ignored, as the kids simply do not know what to say. His typical peers want to be kind, and fear upsetting him.

This is understandable, as growing communication differences can make these experiences complicated. Wil is not in elementary school anymore. Middle schoolers talk and process information more quickly. Wil feels lost in this sea of back-and-forth communication, and a toss of a spoon or messing up someone's hair brings it to a halt. The attention is brought back to Wil. In response, they are kind and think, "Oh that's just Wil."

If a dialogue is started with Wil about why his actions are not respectful to friends, his attention will wander and before you are done talking, he'll have tossed your spoon again. If the reaction is instead to get upset with Wil, he may cry or shut down. He will hear the anger and take it as an attack on his person rather than as a correction to his behavior. A straightforward and firm, "Please do not do that. That's my spoon, I was eating with it." Or "Please do not mess my hair. I don't like it," are more effective. He'll understand your boundaries in just a few short and direct words. It's possible he may try again, but it will end the behavior sooner. Most importantly, setting these direct boundaries with Wil is respecting him as a peer.

This is one of the many ways Wil's relationship with his sisters is very beneficial. Basically, they don't put up with his crap. If he does something like talking with his mouth full, Katherine will say, "Wil, that is gross. Babies do that."

"I'm not a baby!" he will yell back. But on his next bite, he'll chew with his mouth closed.

Katherine and Elizabeth are also very good at changing the direction Wil is going in if he repeats a behavior over and over. When Wil is on a walk, he will find every big stick he can and show it to his sisters. Katherine and Elizabeth will ooooh and ahhhh at first—then growing tired of it, Elizabeth will ask Wil to race her. In that way, he learns boundaries just as naturally as anyone else does.

Just this morning, Wil gave me a hug and started messing with my hair. I pulled out of his hug, looked at him, and said, "Wil, I love your hugs. But please do not mess with my hair, or anyone's hair. People don't like that."

"Ok, Mom." He stopped messing with my hair and gave me another hug. He will likely mess with my hair again on another occasion when he's feeling feisty. I will again say the same thing in the same way. Eventually he will stop doing it. It can take multiple reminders before he decides to respect those boundaries. Sometimes it takes just one. But the important point is that the boundaries need to be set.

Wil's middle school and Connect friends are learning how to set boundaries with him, and he is learning how to respect them. What it comes down to is mutual respect amongst peers, no matter what their similarities or differences are. This Connect program carries with it the essential life skills of working with varying abilities and personalities with care, firmness, kindness, and respect. And these friends are proving what a great time you can have doing just that.

Bat Mitzvah Dance

It was nine in the morning and Wil was jamming to Luke Bryan. That was not unusual. The fact that it was that late in the morning was unusual.

The previous night, Wil, Katherine, Elizabeth, and I went to a dear friend's Bat Mitzvah. The 13-year-old girl of honor, Lila, is in 7th grade with Wil and one of his closest friends. It was the first Bat Mitzvah the kids and I have attended. Prior to the celebration, Lila's mother asked if Wil would prefer to sit with his sisters and me, or at the table with his friends. This was a very considerate question, as she knows Wil can be overwhelmed in large groups and wanted to make sure he was comfortable. Wil's independence has recently grown in leaps and bounds. Last year, I would have answered that he should sit at the table with me. Entering the room would be a big question mark given the noise level of a large group of people and a DJ playing music. (It's a challenge to get Wil to sit down at his sister's basketball games. But if I pull up a chair at the very upper level of the gymnasium, with his noise-cancelling headphones on, Wil will sit and watch the game. The buzzer is too loud and unpredictable for him. I cannot yet talk him into walking down to sit in the bleachers. At this point, coaxing him in to the gymnasium with his knowledge of unpredictable noises is a victory. Sitting in the bleachers will come.)

I knew, when Wil entered the large room at the Bat Mitzvah, he would see the circle of girls that are his friends. Sitting at a table with these girls would not only be a huge feeling of independence for him, but also a lot of fun. I knew he would want nothing to do with me or his sisters when he saw his friends. Anticipating this, I responded to Lila's mom to please seat him with his friends, and she said she'd put me at a neighboring table, just in case. Perfect. When we walked through the lobby into the room where the Bat Mitzvah was being held, Wil immediately saw his friends and ran off with them, as I had hoped and predicted. The music was playing, softer at that point, and he went in without even the slightest hesitation. No noise-cancelling headphones were needed. When it was time to eat, he sat down at the table with his friends and looked around like he was sitting with royalty. And he was. These girls are friends of gold. They encourage Wil, they support Wil, they understand Wil, and they are patient when he needs his space. In turn, he gives them his utmost affection and friendship.

Wil dug into his salad when it was served, and the only time I walked over to his table was when the chicken arrived. I knew he'd need some help cutting it, and I asked the friend seated next to him if she'd help him, or if she preferred that I did. She said she had it covered. Perfect. The only time I saw discomfort in Wil at the table was when the DJ stopped playing music and made the announcements of the celebration—the noise of the microphone had Wil slightly ducking his head. He was holding strong though, because he loved being at that table. There was no way he was going to change that. I made sure I didn't give it any attention. When the announcements were over and the music played again, Wil lifted his head and got back to enjoying time with his friends.

When the dinner plates were cleared and the dancing started, the night was just beginning for Wil. He danced, and danced, and danced. Then danced again. It was the most beautiful thing to see. All of the kids together, dancing, jumping, twisting, turning, having the time of their lives, and there was Wil, right there with them. All as one. The dance floor was common ground.

When Wil was younger, I used to wonder what he would be like if he didn't have Down syndrome. He's a good athlete now, but what kind of athlete would he be without 47 chromosomes? He's an adorable kid, but what would he look like if he didn't have 47 chromosomes? He's a smart guy, but how smart would he be if he didn't have 47 chromosomes? It's natural to wonder. I don't wonder like that anymore. As natural as it is to wonder, it's also natural for those thoughts to fade as you grow with those 47 chromosomes. Wil is Wil. He's whole as he is. And still, seeing the separation between his abilities and his typical peers' abilities is a challenging part of this journey. I'm always seeking a common ground where Wil and his peers can come together as one. The dance floor at Lila's Bat Mitzvah was exactly that place.

A friend, who now lives in Florida but came into town for Lila's Bat Mitzvah, walked over to my table and we started chatting. Her son has autism, and I've known him since he was very young. He and Wil were in preschool together. "Look at Wil," she said. "He gives me hope." Our eyes both filled with tears. Though our sons have their differences, we share a common ground in understanding. Unlike a middle ground, that implies someone must step down, I view a common ground as a place where we all step up—to meet each other at a higher understanding.

Wil and his friends continued dancing and dancing. Wil never once sat down, but after a few hours, he finally decided he better hit the bathroom. When he was inside, one of his favorite songs came on—"Knockin' Boots" by Luke Bryan. After he exited the bathroom, he sprinted faster than Carl Lewis back to the dance floor. About a half hour after "Knockin' Boots," Wil showed signs of slowing down. But Wil doesn't really slow down. He dashes, then comes to an abrupt halt. What seems spontaneous to us has been building over time in him. He bolted off the dance floor into the lobby, then plopped down on a couch in the corner. I sat down next to him, but he turned his head away from me. "What a great time, Wil. And with your friends. Are you getting tired now?" "Hmph," came the reply.

"Does that mean you'd like to go, or do you want to stay?" "Hmph." "If you are ready to go, let's say thank you to Lila and her parents." He looked at me and said, "Ok." He got up and we walked back into the party room. He went immediately to Lila's dad and gave him a big hug. He did the same with Lila's mom. Then he walked over to Lila and gave her a hug. He said good-bye to his friends. Then, without another word, he sprinted from the room into the lobby. I thought he'd go to the couch in the corner again, but when I followed him into the lobby, he wasn't there. I took a quick look around the lobby. The door to the parking lot! I ran out the door, and there he was, walking to the car <heart skips a beat>. "Wil! This is dangerous. Do not go out without me," I said as I ran up to him. I took his hand. "We need to go back in and get your sisters." "No, the car, Mom." I knew by his tone he would not walk back into the lobby. If I forced him, he'd plop on the ground. Fortunately, one of Elizabeth's friends was standing right by the lobby door. I asked her to tell Elizabeth and Katherine to meet me in the car with Wil. She went inside to deliver my message while Wil and I walked to the car. I pulled the car up to the lobby area just as Katherine and Elizabeth were walking out. "Sorry, guys, Wil bolted," I said. "Yeah, I figured that's what happened," Elizabeth replied.

"Would you mind waiting in the car while I say good-bye?" I asked. "Sure." "Thank you! Be right back." I went inside and said good-bye to our wonderful hosts and friends.

"Wil is going to sleep well tonight," they said. And he did. When he woke, he started the party back up again on his CD player with "Knockin' Boots." A good party never ends.

When It's Right, Give A Sprite

During Katherine's hour at CrossFit, Elizabeth, Wil and I grocery shopped. I wasn't feeling that well (some winter bug), so my intention was to make it a quick stop. We picked up the necessary items for dinner, then got into the grocery line. As we waited, Wil spied a Sprite in the cooler.

"Look Mom. Sprite!" Wil said.

"Yes Wil, you love Sprite."

He walked toward the cooler. I put my hand on his shoulder to stop him.

"Not tonight, Wil. Remember, Sprite is your reward for riding the bus home after school. If you would like a water, I'll buy you one. Would you like a water?"

"No. Sprite."

"Wil, if you'd like a drink, water is your choice. We are saving Sprite as your reward for riding the bus after school."

"Yes, Mom, I ride the bus." He said this very seriously. If Wil is having a challenging day at school, he'll refuse to ride the bus. It's a form of control over his situation. His teachers and I are working to develop the habit of him riding the bus. When Wil does choose to ride the bus, he feels great pride in his independence. He bursts in the back door, calling out to me proudly, "Mom, I rode the bus!" Though I'm not a fan of soft drinks, right now I'm following the "whatever works" policy. And what currently works is his knowledge of a Sprite waiting for him in the fridge when he gets off the bus.

"Yes, you do ride the bus, Wil," I said, still holding his shoulder. "I'm very proud of you for doing that. Sprite is for after the bus. Tonight, your choice is water."

He pondered this for a moment. In such a situation, it was very possible that he would decide to dig his heels in about the Sprite, which meant he would go for the cooler against my protest. If I held him back, he would sit on the floor on the spot and refuse to move. If I tried to move him, he would kick or push me away. He's getting too big for me to pick up. Even so, if I attempted to pick him up, he'd get extremely upset and cry. A sobbing, body-shaking kind of cry. It's about more than not getting what he wants—it's about feeling out of control of his situation.

My hand still on Wil's shoulder, I leaned over to Elizabeth and said quietly, "If this starts to blow up, I'll give you my keys to walk Wil to the car." She nodded knowingly. We've been through this before.

"Wil, how about we take a walk across the aisles and see what kinds of water they have? Elizabeth, would you mind waiting in line while Wil and I pick out a water?"

"Sure," Elizabeth replied.

Wil agreed to this, so we walked across the numbered aisles and peered through the glass of their accompanying coolers. When Wil chose a bottle of water that appealed to him, we walked back and met up with Elizabeth in line. It was all gloriously uneventful.

If Wil had refused and it had turned into a full blown plop-on-the-floor-on-the-spot-and-not-move situation, our best choice would have been to wait it out. The last time we went to the grocery store, I gave Wil the choice of whether he wanted to go with Katherine, Elizabeth, and me, or stay home with his dad. Wil said he wanted to go with us to the grocery store. However, when we arrived, he refused to get out of the car. Elizabeth offered to wait with him in the car while Katherine and I went in to shop.

I don't always know the reasoning behind his refusals. Sometimes he's simply tired. Sometimes there is something about the situation that overwhelms him that I'm unaware of. Sometimes it's a matter of exerting his independence. A friend shared a technique with me where Wil and I would count back from 10 together and then make a new choice. That worked at one point, but does not work now. Sometimes I can reason with him. Sometimes I can't. We live a life of "sometimes" and "whatever works" with Wil. Yet even though this sounds contradictory, as there are so many variables to Wil's actions, consistency is key when responding to him. I can't say yes to a Sprite on one occasion, and then say no on another. That's extremely confusing for him. Though right now we are in a "sometimes" and "whatever works" situation with Wil, I must be consistent. It's also important to give him the time to make a choice, whether he makes that choice by sitting on the floor, staying in the car, or walking to the coolers in the grocery store.

Wil requires extra time to process what his next step will be, and every single one of us has the need to know we have choices. Rush Wil and you are asking to set yourself back even further. I found Wil's decision to walk with me from aisle to aisle looking for water to be a sign of maturity. He was thinking beyond his immediate gratification. Wil reasoned through his choices and valued the meaning of a reward in the future.

Milestones with Wil are rarely smooth to emerge. They take a lot of patience and trial and error. So when signs of independence arrive like last night, they are never overlooked or easily taken for granted. I know Elizabeth and Katherine see this too. I have no doubt it's challenging at times for them to have the patience they do with their brother. Their patience with his "sometimes" behavior applies everywhere we go. And still, it's their norm. It's what they do. Elizabeth has said to me on a number of occasions, "I just don't understand why people can't accept people just as they are."

Give that girl a Sprite!

Common Bridges

"Come on, you have your ear protectors on. It will be fun. Remember you wanted to go to the movies?" I asked Wil.

Katherine, Elizabeth, and I were juggling popcorn buckets and drink cups in the hallway just outside the entrance to the theater room where "Frozen 2" would be playing. Wil sat on the floor, smack dab in the center of the entrance. We had made it through the lobby with very few signs of resistance from Wil. Then he came to a sudden, abrupt halt. Looking back, there were a few small red flags. When I ordered popcorn, Wil said he didn't want any <red flag>. I ordered him a small bucket and a soda knowing he would change his mind. When we reached the soda fountain, he perked up. He willingly reached up to press the button on the fountain to choose his drink and filled his cup to the top. He was one happy guy holding his cup walking down the hallway <red flag down!>.

All four of us walked down the hallway to the theater room with our treats, when Wil plopped on the ground. And there we were.

"Wil if you aren't going in, can you at least scoot to the side so people don't have to walk around you to get into the movie?" I said.

Three boys sat on a couch against a wall in the hallway. They were staring at us. I'm used to the stares. And in a way, they are a good thing. Everyone has their own version of normal. Our version was clearly different from that of the boys on the couch, or they wouldn't be staring. The more we observe other people's "normal," the greater chance we have to understand them. I hoped those boys were getting an education as I talked to Wil. Wil scooted across the floor away from the entrance.

"Thank you, Wil. So what is going on here? It's not that loud in there. And I have your noise-cancelling headphones right here. You were very excited to see "Frozen 2." Can you help me understand why you won't go in?" I received no response from Wil, though I really didn't expect one at this point.

"Olaf is so funny. I can't wait to see him in the movie. Hey, we might even laugh 'til we wet our pants. How about that!" Wil looked up at me with the faintest smile, like he really wanted to laugh, then put his head back down. He wasn't ready to be that open yet.

"Is it the popcorn? You don't have to eat it." I said.

The previews started rolling and Katherine wanted to go in to watch them.

"Mom, I can carry in Wil's popcorn and soda," Katherine said.

"Thank you, Katherine."

Katherine enveloped both her and Wil's popcorn buckets in her arms with drinks in each hand. She then made her way into the theater. I thought of all the times Katherine and Elizabeth need to be patient in situations such as this. They take it in stride. This is their "normal." Elizabeth stayed in the hallway with me to help encourage Wil into the theater. People were streaming by us, but Wil remained un-phased by the traffic and the boys staring from the couch. Elizabeth worked on convincing Wil to enter the theater by asking him questions. She received very little response. For whatever reason, Wil resists piggyback rides from any of us except Elizabeth, so she asked, "Wil, do you want a piggyback ride?"

Wil weighs 104 pounds, but Elizabeth was up for the task. Wil stood up and I breathed a sigh of relief. I helped him onto Elizabeth's back, put on his noise-cancelling headphones, and we all made our way to our seats. Wil crossed a mental barrier as much as a physical one when we entered that room. He laughed as he reclined his seat. He then asked to hold his popcorn and placed his drink in the cup holder. And we did laugh at Olaf, but thankfully evaded any pants-wetting.

The previous week, when Wil and I went to the same theater for a Down Syndrome Support Team event, there were multiple other kids with Down syndrome who also decided that they did not want to enter the room where the movie was being shown. My guess is they were full of excitement just as Wil was, but when at the threshold, they found some part of the experience overwhelming.

Be it an unfamiliar room or concern of loud noises, without the verbal communication skills to express these emotions, physical communication is used instead—in the form of coming to a complete stop. On this particular occasion, Wil entered the theater without incident. However, I fully understood what was happening with the kids seated at the threshold of the room, as did everyone else in our Down Syndrome Support Team. There were no stares. This group of parents and siblings have all been there, done that. It is our "normal."

When Wil was very young, we were part of a playgroup held at a school for children under 5 years old. When Wil developed the ability to run, his favorite pastime was to find the door and escape down the hallway as quickly as he could. I had to watch him like a hawk or he would disappear in the blink of an eye. If he did escape, I'd leave Katherine and Elizabeth with a friend while I sprinted out the door to chase Wil down the hallway. He was the only child who did that, with very few exceptions. Most of the children were content at that age to play together or with the multitude of the toys in the room. Not Wil. His favorite pastime was to escape at any chance he could find.

I started hosting Down Syndrome Support Team play dates at about this same time. Though there were many toys and activities, most of the children there did as Wil did—spent their time planning their escape to run down the hallway. As challenging as it was for all of us mothers, I also found it hugely comforting to be in an environment where this behavior was the norm.

Katherine, Elizabeth, and I recently went shopping with Wil. We all know that our time is limited when shopping with him, as he will run off or take a seat in the middle of the store when he's tired. We watch for the cues. It's a team effort. We went to one store, and I took him for a walk while Katherine and Elizabeth shopped and tried on outfits. Wil and I would circle back around to where the girls were shopping so I could see what they liked, or answer a question, then we'd circle around again. We made it through that store without incident. Then we headed to one other store. We tried the same tactic, but I could tell Wil was falling apart. He started running and taking off. I saw a friend, Julie, shopping with her daughter. I waved and said hello as I followed the top of Wil's head through the aisles of clothes. She called out to me, "How are you doing?"

"You know, just chasing Wil as per usual!" Julie knows Wil, has four kids of her own, and is a teacher. She nodded her head in understanding and smiled. She gets this kind of "normal."

Following Wil, I ran into Elizabeth. I told her we had limited time—that Wil had reached his limit. Elizabeth said that was fine, she didn't see anything she liked anyway and was ready to go. We walked together, following Wil, to give Katherine some extra shopping time. For whatever reason, during Wil's running, he decided he wanted a vest. A $250 North Face vest. He pulled it off the rack to show it to me. I agreed it was really cool, because it was. But he was not getting a $250 vest, as cool as it was. He was not happy with that and decided to run around the store again.

When Wil gets like this, I prefer he stay on the move, because if he drops on the floor, it's really hard to get him back up again. The flip side is, he can easily decide to run out the door.

Elizabeth and I both looked at each other and telepathically communicated it was time to go. Elizabeth said, "I'll text Katherine to meet us at the car."

I told Wil we were leaving and he made a sprint to the door. I put my arm around his shoulders and slowed him to a walk.

"Why your arm on me, Mom?" Wil asked.

"Because we are headed to the parking lot and we need to be safe."

"So I'm not flat like a pancake."

"Exactly."

We made it to the car, then off to lunch. It was time for us all to sit in one place and enjoy some downtime together, which is exactly what we did.

Elizabeth came home from school one day and shared with me that her health teacher, Mrs. April Stewart, sat down with her and a few other friends. Elizabeth said there was some downtime in the class, so Mrs. Stewart shared some stories about her sister with Down syndrome. Elizabeth said they laughed about the similarities between Mrs. Stewart's sister and Elizabeth's brother. How they could be very headstrong, but also openly and unconditionally loving. Elizabeth told me how special these conversations were to her. Elizabeth said, "You really can't understand what it's like to have a brother with Down syndrome and it's hard to explain. But Mrs. Stewart really understands. I also like that the others in the group hear these stories so they can understand, too."

Elizabeth said Mrs. Stewart had tears in her eyes talking about her sister. That she really misses her. I had tears in my eyes too after Elizabeth shared this with me. (April and I met at a basketball meeting for our daughters, Elizabeth and Maggie. April saw Wil running around the gym and asked if he was my son. She then shared she had a sister with Down syndrome. We instantly became friends.)

In many ways, I feel like we live in two different worlds: the typical world and the Down syndrome world. In our Down syndrome world, what Wil does is completely normal behavior. The stops at the movie theater entrance when it all feels too much. Or the sprints out the door when the shopping has gone on too long. But Wil has two typical sisters and we live in a typical world, so we must balance the two. Wherever we go, we must be prepared. It's always a guessing game of how long Wil will last, as we watch for the cues that he's tired. Because the typical world moves much faster, is a lot louder, and has much less patience than the Down syndrome world. In the Down syndrome world, we stop when we feel overwhelmed. Or we bolt because it's much more appealing to run down an open hallway than to be overstimulated by the multitudes of activity crowded into one room. In the typical world, we crave this activity—more is better. We seek distraction, and we try to pack in as much as we can in a very short time.

It is a delicate dance to balance the two worlds. Katherine and Elizabeth understand this dance and they do it very well. I'm always amazed at how well they roll with the circumstances and we make it all work as a team. I'm thankful for the Mrs. Stewarts in our lives. It's of great importance for Katherine and Elizabeth to know others who balance these two worlds.

These friends are our bridges—where our varying "normals" are broad and in-between. A place we can laugh and cry together with no explanations needed, because our understanding is whole on this well-traversed common ground.

Navigating The Methods of Plane Sailing

"The gate is closing in four minutes, ma'am," an airline representative said to me as I sat on the floor with Wil.

"Yes, thank you," I said. "I just can't get him up. I'm trying."

I saw Wil falling apart about thirty minutes prior to the airline representative's four-minute gate closing alert. When it started in his mind, I can't tell you. The physical signs of his shoulders beginning to slump as he muttered to himself were my cues that things were going downhill within him. My guess was what started as excitement for our trip to Florida had transitioned into overwhelm for him. It's not that he didn't want to go—it was the opposite. The anticipation of all there was ahead of him became too much. He'd see my parents, he'd swim in their pool, he'd go to the beach. He loves my parents dearly and the thought of swimming every day was something he'd been excitedly talking about—especially after being homebound for so long with the pandemic. The building anticipation about all there was to do and see was brewing into the perfect storm. Unfortunately, I only had four minutes left to quell it.

When I saw the first signs of Wil starting to shut down I enlisted Elizabeth's help, as she typically jokes with him and is able to turn his mood around. She told me she was noticing the same signs in Wil. She knew something was happening within him and it would soon go downhill fast. Katherine was reading a book at the time, so I explained what Elizabeth and I saw happening. I asked if she wouldn't mind standing by the bags while Elizabeth and I attempted to understand what was happening with Wil. She agreed.

Elizabeth and I began trying to perk Wil up first with jokes, then by sharing stories about seeing Grandma Leigh and Grandpa in Florida. As we talked to him, the line of passengers boarding the plane shortened. Time was running out. With Wil, though, time is what we need on our side. Despite our efforts, he slumped down further. I knew if Wil sat on the ground we'd likely not get him back up. I scanned the room and saw an empty wheelchair owned by the airline. A passenger had used it to board first class and now no longer needed it. I quickly ran over to retrieve the wheelchair and rolled it next to Wil.

"Look Wil! Do you want to go for a ride?" I asked. He looked up at the wheelchair, then down again. Nothing in my arsenal was working. We've been down similar roads with Wil before. Each time, we needed time. Then it happened—Wil sat down on the floor. What I did next is not what I wanted, but at that moment I could think of no other options.

"Elizabeth, we have to lift him up. Can you help me?" The two of us lifted Wil and he adamantly refused. The passengers remaining in line to board the plane began to stare. They knew nothing of the build-up of this moment; that Elizabeth and I had been trying to lift Wil's mood for nearly thirty minutes. The snapshot of time they observed was the force being used. I felt simultaneously sad and angry; not at the passengers, not at Wil, but at myself. How could I, the mother, force my son against his will? What message did this send to Wil? What message did this send to his sisters? What message did this send to the outside world? That force is the answer? But the problem was I didn't know the answer. I simply didn't know what to do in that short window of time to get Wil on the plane. I did know he needed time to process. I did know he needed time to tell me what was upsetting him. I did know, with time, that he would stand on his own and board the plane. The problem was, the plane would be long gone with the time Wil required. Thus, I resorted to lifting Wil into the wheelchair, which he would then slide out of back onto the ground.

When the gate to the plane was nearly closed, I was sweating, frustrated, and on the verge of tears. I racked my brain for options: Elizabeth and Katherine could board this flight themselves. They would be 15 years old in a few days and had been on this flight many times. Wil and I would board the next available flight to Florida. But when would the next available flight be? A few hours? The next day? I knew how incredibly distraught Wil would be when the plane left without us. But how could I penalize Katherine and Elizabeth by making them stay back, too?

As these thoughts swirled through my brain, Elizabeth and I continued our final attempts to get Wil in the wheelchair. Moments before the gate closed, one of the airline representatives walked over and bent down to Wil's level on the floor. "Can you get in the chair –" she paused and looked at me.

"Wil," I said, "his name is Wil."

"Wil, can you get in the chair?" He looked up at the airline representative. She was a break in his pattern; he was no longer fighting me or his sister. Hers was a fresh, new face. I took a deep breath full of hope. Please, please, please, I prayed.

"We are going to see his grandparents. He's very excited for all the swimming he'll be doing," I said to the airline representative, so she'd have more personal information to persuade Wil.

"Wil, don't you want to go swimming?" She asked. "And to see your grandparents? Let's get you in the chair so you can do that."

Wil stood, and I felt as if a 110-pound weight was lifted off my shoulders. In a way, it was. Wil sat in the chair and the airline representative wheeled him to the gate. I then took the handles, and as I did, I looked her in the eyes and said, "Thank you." She looked back at me and nodded. I couldn't tell if she understood what was happening or if she thought I was an awful person for forcing my child against his will. Either way, I was immensely grateful for her help, and that she gave our family the gift of boarding the plane together.

One challenge of raising awareness is that the moment of time observed is rarely the full picture. When I saw Wil physically starting to spiral downward, it was over thirty minutes prior to the gates closing, and what was happening in his mind likely started sooner than that. But what the outside world saw was the five-minute breakdown. What message was received in that short five minutes to contribute to or take away from Down syndrome awareness? It's rarely a black-and-white answer. Rather, it's a process that happens over time, with loads of gray areas. Though I've been raising Wil for 13 years, every day I navigate a new shade of gray.

Once we boarded the plane, Wil was back to his silly, fun-loving self. We had crossed whatever barrier was in his mind. During our flight to Florida, I was already mentally preparing for the flight back home. I thought back over the signs of Wil breaking down—when they happened, how they happened, what happened before the signs, what our conversations had been in preparation for the flight, and so on. What options could I use to prevent this from happening again? When it was time for the flight back home, my mom packed Wil's favorite snacks. I downloaded some of his favorite movies and television shows. My mom bought him new miniature toy cars he could play with on the plane. My dad talked to him about how great his flight home would be. We didn't need a single one of our prepared options as Wil breezed through security and onto the plane without a single halt. It was all gloriously uneventful.

Though it has come and gone, the airport incident stays with me. It's a puzzle to unfold. A puzzle successfully unfolded with extra time, but what to do when extra time is not a given? Force is not the answer. Domineering someone is not the answer. Anticipation and preparation are *part* of the answer, as are experience and learning to read Wil's cues more accurately. As I continue to discover and uncover more answers, I know—now more than ever—that when I do have the gift of time, I need to take a deep breath and take it.

The day after we arrived back home, I decided to make a Costco trip, as our cupboards were bare. Katherine and Elizabeth love Costco trips. We had not been there since the pandemic, so the girls were extra excited at the prospect. Earlier that morning, Wil had gone with me to the school to return his sisters' Chromebooks and textbooks, as school just ended for the summer. We saw his speech therapist and he enjoyed a conversation with her. Wil missed seeing his teachers in person during the pandemic, so this was a real treat. He was in great spirits, so I was surprised when he immediately turned down the prospect of going to Costco.

"Wil, you love their pizza. Remember those huge slices of pizza?" His answer was still no.

As both Katherine and Elizabeth were looking forward to the Costco trip, I wasn't about to ask one of them to stay home with Wil. So the question was, how did I convince Wil to go? I knew in time, I could figure out what Wil's roadblock to going to Costco was. Unlike the airport incident, the gift of time was on my side.

"So, Wil, why don't you want to go to Costco?"

"Humpf." (His favorite answer when he doesn't want to explain.)

"Wil, aren't you hungry? It's been awhile since you had breakfast."

"Yeeeeeeees," he said and looked at me. His sense of humor was there. A great sign!

"Sooooo," I said mimicking his drawn out "yes." "Let's go to Costco." And I did a little dance.

"Mom, you are silly," he said, laughing.

"I know, so are you. Let's go silly." I tickled him.

Elizabeth heard the exchange and came into Wil's room. "Suddenly I feel very tired," she said. "I'm going to take a nap." Elizabeth sprawled out on Wil's bed. This is a regular joke between them.

"No," Wil said and jumped on Elizabeth. "This is not Lizbeth's bed!" Elizabeth fake snored. "Lizbeth get up." Elizabeth continued to fake snore and Wil bounced on her. "I'll go on Lizbeth's bed." Wil got up and ran toward her bedroom.

"Hey, not my bed!" Elizabeth jumped up and chased him.

"Yes, your bed," Wil said. Elizabeth bear hugged him before he reached her bedroom and turned him around. They both fell down laughing.

"Ok Wil, let's go to Costco," Elizabeth said.

"No!" Wil ran back to his room. I thanked Elizabeth for trying, then went back to Wil's room. I sat down next to him. He picked up his iPad and started playing a game. I sat with him awhile. After some time and discussion about his game, I tried again.

"Wil, what's the problem? You love Costco pizza. It will be a fun trip."

He was quiet, so I waited him out. Then I asked him again.

"Too long of a trip, Mom," he replied.

I remained calm and nodded my head, but inside I was doing cartwheels. He didn't simply respond yes or no. He told me why! He told me what he was thinking and why he didn't want to go! All it took was giving him the time he needed.

Time is both a challenging and a simple answer to unravel what Wil is thinking inside. It is simple in the fact that when time is extended to him, the answers come. It is challenging in the fact that the time he needs is not always available. When I *do* have time, it can sometimes wear on my patience when time is required over and over again. But when the answers come, they are always worth the time. The milestone of Wil expressing his "why" filled my heart to overflowing. I would wait to the ends of the earth to hear words like that. We parents who experience such milestones know the elation we feel when the milestones emerge seemingly spontaneously, while in reality, under the surface, these milestones have been worked on and waited on diligently and patiently over time. Similar to the airport incident, where many see a snapshot in time, most experiences have an underlying build-up to that moment.

"So that's why you don't want to go? It will take too long?" I asked.

"Yes," he said.

"Ok, how about this?" I asked. "How about we make it a short trip? Then a big slice of pizza at the end of the short trip."

"Ok." Wil stood up and slipped his Crocs on. No fighting, no domineering. Wil's feelings were expressed, heard, and validated. Oh sweet time, how I could hug you!

I was thankful, too, that Katherine and Elizabeth were witness to the process of the Costco trip, and that they saw that the message being sent was the gift of time. I told them I wasn't proud of the incident on the plane, that I still don't know what the right answer was. But I do know, when we have time, Wil needs that time extended to him. To unwind, to unfold, to process. How would we feel if people were always running over us with their agenda? That's likely how he feels *all* the time. It not about giving him what he wants all the time. It's about giving him the time to tell us what he wants and how he feels, so he knows he's heard.

When we arrived at Costco, Wil wouldn't get out of the car. I reminded him that he had agreed to a short trip. Katherine and Elizabeth joked with him. Katherine and Elizabeth tickled him. Katherine and Elizabeth eventually urged him out of the car. The patience these girls have with most things we do is their norm. We rarely just get in the car and go somewhere. There is always the element of time required. I expressed to the girls that I know it can be tiring to always be extending extra time to Wil, and that they are wonderful at making that extra time fun. When we make the challenges fun, the joy on the other end is bigger. Just like the big ol' slice of pizza at the end of the Costco trip. Wil held his up like a king.

Elizabeth has said, "There are good days, bad days, and Wil days." Her sentiment sums this up beautifully. Acceptance of the WHOLE. Every day is new, and I learn from each one of them. When I know better, I do better. As Wil has proved, uncovering the "why" behind it all is the joy of a lifetime, no matter how much time it takes.

I'm thankful to know *all* of the days, and my deep breath of hope is, that you are too.

R-Word Value

Last night the word "retard" was said on a television show Elizabeth and I were watching. We both reflexively flinched.

"Why did they even say that?" Elizabeth asked.

"It wasn't needed at all."

Word, sister! Can you imagine having to prove the value of your child? The mere fact your child was born with one tiny extra chromosome leaves you in that position. To show the world he is not "less than" when every stereotype suggests otherwise. My son is not the subject of a joke on TV. The defenses of your child's value go up even before he's born.

If a diagnosis of Down syndrome is given during prenatal testing, many will share words of sympathy with you rather than congratulations. Isn't the fact that he is a human being born into this life miracle enough? But sadly, it's not enough. So when hurtful comments like those on a television show occur, I am reminded not to let my guard down. That even though my immediate community is supportive of Wil and who he is as an individual, there is much work to be done outside of our community.

Should I be expected to prove my son's value to you? Should I be expected to prove my son's value to television show writers who carelessly degrade him with words projected to the masses? Should I be expected to prove my son's value to new moms; to women who are about to give birth and know very little about Down syndrome? Should I be expected to prove my son's value to those who utter words of sympathy when we deserve their words of congratulations instead? The very fact these questions exist is proof of the need to share our stories. Sharing stories about our loved ones with Down syndrome is not optional; it is integral. Sharing stories opens the gateways of understanding, which in turn deflate the meaning of ignorant jokes. Sharing stories creates personal connections and eliminates the fear of the unknown. Sharing stories opens minds to a beautiful life that counts beyond the number of chromosomes. Sharing stories is the answer to questions we should never be expected to ask in the first place.

Elizabeth was right—hurtful words are never needed. But our stories are essential.

A BROADER VIEW

Special Olympics

When you go to a Special Olympics event, there are athletes who talk to themselves or break out in song. There are athletes who decide they are done before the event is over and sit right down on the spot. There are athletes who spin in circles, who hold on to items for comfort, and who make a point to talk to every observer. There are athletes who are downright competitive. And there is a volunteer to support every type of athlete.

Most of these athletes live in a world not made for them, and are constantly learning to function in that world. The Special Olympics is a place to relax some of those boundaries. To work at their natural level. In this environment, the athletes have the freedom to learn, grow, and showcase their many talents—then to enjoy the fun part of celebrating those talents.

When you go to a Special Olympics event, you may also find parents spinning, breaking out in song, and sitting down on a grassy hill soaking in the scenery. We find this experience just as freeing, as we too navigate a world not made for our children.

Remember To Check The Enthusiasm Gauge

We are busy. Much too busy. The online self-help bookshelves at Amazon cover multitudes of pages. How to best use our time. How to organize. How to relieve stress. How to be our best selves. There are therapists for any ailment and drugs that advertise relief from whatever ails you. With so many tools available, why do so many seem as stressed as ever? It's like a competition to see who is busier.

I overheard a conversation while waiting in the check-out line at a grocery store. Two ladies ran into each other, and soon they were competing over who had had less sleep. Is that really a competition you want to win? It seems that being busy is supposed to win us a gold star. And yet, there is a vast difference between being busy and being purposeful. How purposeful are we really being in our busyness? Are we missing the point as we run in circles?

We seem busier, but unhappier. I don't believe there are any secrets, but I do believe there are methods for being happier and more purposeful in life. It does involve making some difficult changes in how you approach life and who you surround yourself with. Each and every time I attend a Special Olympics event, my happiness quotient goes up. It's because of both the participants *and* the volunteers. When you are communicating with someone with varying needs, you need to first understand their communication style.

Most of us typical folks adapt to a certain style of communication even if it isn't our preferred way of speaking and learning. But you can't speak to a child with Down syndrome rapidly and expect them to process everything you are saying. You can't tell them to hurry up when they don't want to. It ain't gonna happen. Believe me, I've tried. If you speak to a child with autism in generalities, you will have a very upset and frustrated child on your hands. It's important to slow down and consider who you are talking to. You have to consider your audience and how to convey your message from their perspective.

Now, that may sound stressful to you, and at times it can be. But here's the secret… this process lifts you up above all the noise in your head and places you on a different plane. This process broadens your perspective, which is another key to happiness.

At a recent Special Olympics function, I was sitting on the side of a hill with a few of the athletes. I struck up a conversation with two of them I was sitting next to. One of the athletes told me he works at a nursing home. He stuttered in his explanation, but that did not slow down his enthusiasm in explaining to me how he cleans floors, makes beds, takes care of general room clean-up, and the many friends he's made. I barely needed to ask a question before he was answering it. I felt lifted by this conversation. I actually found myself on the edge of happy tears. I'm sure it was in part due to seeing this young man thrive, as Wil will be a young adult in six years. My happiness was also attributed to the ease of sitting on the grass on a summer day listening to a young man tell me how much he enjoyed his work. He wasn't telling me how stressed he was to clean the floors, or how some coworker was an absolute jerk, or how he hadn't slept in three days. He was a man grateful for his daily life and couldn't wait to tell me all about it. I want to be more like him.

Sorry, ladies in the grocery store line competing over lack of sleep—my new friend is the adulthood winner. We fill most of our days with so much busyness, that it clouds out any ounce of enthusiasm for what we're doing. I'm not saying that we do not have very important things to attend to. That our stressors aren't heavy. But what I *am* saying is that the key to happiness is to step back and take a really good look at what we are doing. To find the purpose in what we are doing. To find the value in what we are doing. To ask ourselves if we are winning the busy battle or the purposeful battle. Our busyness or purposefulness gauge is our level of enthusiasm.

I'm always thankful for my time at Special Olympics events. We could all use the time to step back and assess how to meet our own special needs.

Sharing The Lane

I emerged from the ladies' locker room into the pool area, and as always, held my breath. I made a quick scan of the pool. I exhaled in relief to see an open lane. I wouldn't have to share. Over 2 yards of width and 25 yards of length lined off for my very own self—a swimmer's heaven. I claimed my lane by setting down my gear, took a seat on the edge of the pool, and dangled my legs in the water. As I pulled on my cap and goggles, I saw a man walk in, and thought, "I may have to share now."

He walked by me, smiled and said, "I like your suit." That gave me a twinge of guilt over my selfishness.

"Thank you," I replied. He moved on and walked up to the lifeguard sitting in his tall chair. He struck up a conversation with the lifeguard, who seemed to already know him. Clearly, this man was a regular here.

My times at the pool, while consistent in the number of days, are erratic in the time of day. Sometimes it's the early afternoon, sometimes the late afternoon or even evening. My days fluctuate with my work and kids' schedules. It was about 9AM and I had not yet been to the pool at this time on this day of the week.

The man was still chatting it up with the lifeguard when I hopped in the pool. I didn't know if he was just talking until a lane opened up, or if this was the natural length of their conversation each time he visited the pool. Either way, it didn't seem he'd approach me soon to share a lane. I began swimming and the conversation above me instantly muted. My view was clear water edged by rounded white concrete walls. A dark blue tiled line imbedded in the bottom of the pool guided my way. The familiar tingle of chlorinated water hit the bridge of my nose and I stretched into the rhythm of the swim.

About five minutes into my swim, I saw the talkative man's legs enter the water. Someone must have gotten out, which allowed him to take over their lane at the furthest edge of the pool. I could see the man start to swim three lanes over from mine. Now all the lanes were full. We swimmers were lined up, one by one, with our own thoughts, swimming our own way, on our own course.

Not much later, while taking a breath, I saw multiple feet making their way across the pool deck. When I stopped at the end of my interval, the pool area echoed with noise. Men and women, it appeared mainly in their twenties, were ready to enter the pool. Some jumped into the open area, about three lanes wide, while others walked tentatively with floatation devices down the ramp. I heard a woman, who must have been the teacher in the group, say, "Ok <she rattled off a few names>, it looks like you will have to share a lane."

One woman, who had Down syndrome, appeared to be upset by the thought of not having a lane to swim in. She looked very serious about her swimming time. When a lane opened up, three men from the group jumped in together and started swimming and bouncing off the bottom of the pool. The woman waited, scanning the pool, for another lane to open up.

The talkative man who had taken the end lane also saw what was happening. He said to the woman, "You can swim with me if you want. I'll take one side, and you take the other. Which side do you want?" She seemed happy enough with this situation, jumped in, and started swimming.

The woman in the lane directly next to mine came to a stop. We both looked at each other and acknowledged the situation.

"I think we need to share," she said. Her lane was in the open area where the rest of the group was entering. The big group needed that space.

"Yep," I said, "Come on over."

She ducked under the lane line, popped up in my lane, and asked, "Do you want to rotate, or stay on one side?"

"How about I take this side, you take that side?" I proposed.

"Sounds good to me. Thanks," she replied. And we went off on our way.

The rounded white concrete walls now were fanned with legs treading water or jumping up and down in the shallower end. I saw, from underwater, a trepid fellow with a floatation device around his waist inching his way up and down the length of the pool while hugging the edge.

The pool was full now—some swimming laps, some side-paddling, some bouncing off the bottom, some hanging on the edges. We all made space for one another, while also doing our own thing.

Ten minutes hadn't gone by when I saw the talkative man exit the pool. He said to the young woman, "It's all yours now. Have a great swim!" He walked up to the lifeguard and had another conversation, then left.

I don't know if he surrendered his lane because he only planned a shorter swim that day, or if he was kindly giving the young woman her space. Whatever his reasons, his friendliness left a feeling of goodwill in his wake.

After about another 20 minutes, the group of young adults exited the pool. I was swimming, so I didn't immediately see where they dispersed to. I just noticed that the rounded white concrete walls were back to their quiet state.

I then saw about 10 young men from the group of swimmers exit the hot tub and walk together to the men's locker room. These men were clearly friends. They joked with one another and there was a sense of ease about them. I wondered, would this group of men be friends if they were not categorized as young adults with "special needs?" Were they friends because they formed natural friendships within this program? Or were they friends because they have not been included in our current society, and thus this is the only place they find friendship?

I'm extremely thankful this program for young adults with varying needs exists to integrate these young adults into society. What I have found is this: it is the current society that struggles to integrate these young adults. In our current society, we fight for our own lane. It is viewed as taking too much patience on our part to understand others' needs. But in that erroneous thinking, we miss out on learning who these men really are as individuals. We miss out on discovering their values and gifts. Their strengths and weaknesses. All of who they are.

There is room here for all of us to do our thing and share our space at the same time. When we share our space, we send out a ripple of goodwill. When we give of ourselves, we not only learn about one another, but also grow a deeper understanding about ourselves. Our patience grows. Our compassion grows. Our society grows.

Come on over, let's share the lane.

CLOSING STORY:
THIS IS HOW WE ROLL

Learning To Float

Wil's swim instructor was showing him how to roll over from his stomach to his back in the water. Wil would begin face down, body relaxed, floating in the water. His task was to twist himself around to float in a face-up position. As he twisted his body around to the face-up position, he'd flail his arms and kick his legs. He'd pop his head to the surface, his clear-lensed wide-eyed goggles—he affectionately calls "frog power" when he puts them on—revealing his own wide eyes underneath. He'd sputter and spit out water. Then, catching his breath, he'd float on his back, realizing he succeeded—a huge smile spreading across his face.

The instructor encouraged Wil to try again. Again Wil twisted, flailed, and kicked to float in a face-up position. (Wil's low muscle tone makes this task challenging, but helpful for improving his core strength.) Again Wil surfaced, eyes wide, sputtering, spitting out water, catching his breath. He'd find his way to floating face-up and smile. Over and again, his instructor encouraged another try. Wil twisted, flailed, and kicked. Sputtered and spit. Then smiled. With each try, he'd twist with more ease. He'd spit out less water. His smiles came sooner. On his final try, I could see Wil's smile shining underwater. He completed the turn and lay on his back, arms wide, floating and smiling up to the sky.

As I watched this process unfold, I thought to myself, isn't life just like that?

143

ACKNOWLEDGMENTS

It is said that the little things matter most, and I believe that to be true. So, I'd like to start by thanking a little thing—the 3rd copy of the 21st chromosome. To those that carry that little extra, you make the world a better place.

To the families of the Down Syndrome Support Team, you know how big the little things are.

To Cheri Riemer, for your friendship in celebrating the little things fully and knowingly. For the photos on the cover of this book. For your persistent encouragement to complete this book. Without which, this book may never have come to completion.

To Sarah Block, for your editing skills, for your friendship, for our shared love of the oldies. You made a large project doable. And through it all, we remained on the same page. Without you, I'd still be a mixed metaphor sawing away at the words with my nose to the grindstone.

To Brittany Toth, for your creativity, for your kindness, for taking the time to caringly design the cover of this book. You know how to celebrate the little things in a big way.

To Jen Geer, for your eye for detail; for making a photography session fun, natural and easy-going, just as it should be to capture one's true essence.

To Lila Harvey, for writing the foreword to this book. For your family's friendship, for being on "Wil call" at a moment's notice and always taking it in stride.

To Jeff and Leigh, my dad and mom, who are definitely the coolest parents on this planet. I love you to the moon and back.

To Elizabeth and Katherine, my beautiful girls. You are sisters of gold with natures of gold. I'm forever thankful to share this life together with you.

To Matt, my husband, for your love, for making me laugh and for this family we created together.

And to Wil, my beautiful boy. You changed everything and for that, I wouldn't change a thing. You are a bright light in this world. Shine on!

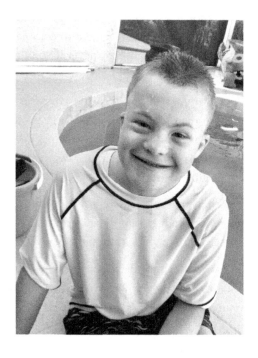

Thank you for sharing your time with us! I look forward to connecting again through more stories as our journey unfolds.

ABOUT THE AUTHOR

Christie Taylor will tell you she writes better than sings, but you still may catch her belting out a tune down a stretch of quiet country road on one of her long runs. Running and writing help Christie gain a fresh perspective and soak in the simple joys of life. Christie began writing stories about her son, Wil, shortly after he was born and diagnosed with Down syndrome. Initially, writing helped Christie sort out her many emotions about navigating life with Down syndrome. With time, Christie found her storytelling connected her with many other families who were raising children with Down syndrome, while at the same time, raising much needed awareness. Christie has run multiple races for the National Down Syndrome Society, and her writings have been published in The Mighty and The Huffington Post. You can view her blogs on www.WILingness.com. Christie lives in Michigan with her husband, Matt; twin daughters, Katherine and Elizabeth; son, Wil; yellow lab, Woody (the best dog in the world); and two cats, Oreo and Grimace (both aptly named).

Made in the USA
Monee, IL
14 July 2020